PROFILES OF HEALING

WALKING THUNDER

Walking Thunder

Diné Medicine Woman

EDITED BY BRADFORD KEENEY, PH.D

Photographs by Kern L. Nickerson

RINGING ROCKS PRESS

in association with

LEETE'S ISLAND BOOKS

PUBLISHED BY

Ringing Rocks Press
P.O. Box 22656
Philadelphia, PA 19110-2656
www.ringingrocks.org

IN ASSOCIATION WITH

Leete's Island Books
Post Office Box 3131
Stony Creek, CT 06405 USA

DISTRIBUTION

Independent Publishers Group
814 North Franklin Street
Chicago, IL 60610 USA
1-800-888-4741 or
www.frontdesk@ipgbook.com

BLACK AND WHITE ARCHIVAL IMAGES

Courtesy Museum of New Mexico
(negative numbers under each
photograph refer to the Museum
of New Mexico's Photo Archives)

COLOR PHOTOGRAPHY

Kern L. Nickerson
Ringing Rocks Foundation © 2001

WITH THE EXCEPTION OF THE FOLLOWING IMAGES:
PAGE 9: ©Mike Howell/ISP
PAGE 114: ©Weatherstock/ISP
PAGE 136: ©Bill Stormont/Stock Market
PAGES 148–149: ©Chad Ehlers/ISP
PAGE 173: ©Michael Agliolo/ISP
PAGE 187: ©Ron Sanford/Stock Market
PAGES 193, 195: Marian Jenson

ILLUSTRATIONS

COVER SYMBOL Enter into Beauty
SYMBOLS & DRAWINGS BY Walking Thunder
(unless otherwise noted in the caption)
MAP, PAGE 10 Peter Seward

DESIGN AND PRODUCTION

Davidson Design, Inc., New York

LIBRARY OF CONGRESS 2001 132113

ISBN 0-918172-30-6 (hardbound)
ISBN 0-918172-32-2 (paperback)

PRINTED IN CHINA

WE WOULD LIKE TO THANK THE FOLLOWING PUBLISHERS AND AUTHORS FOR THEIR PERMISSION TO REPRINT MATERIAL FROM EXISTING PUBLICATIONS:

American Folklore Society; American Museum of Natural History; Columbia University Press; Inner Traditions, Int'l; Oklahoma University Press; The Peabody Museum of Archaeology and Ethnology, Harvard University; Rio Nuevo Publishers; University of New Mexico Press

This is the sixth volume in an ongoing series of books entitled *Profiles of Healing*. The series is a project of the Ringing Rocks Foundation, an organization that supports the survival and future development of global healing wisdom through education, research, and special projects. All volumes are fully illustrated and include an audio CD drawn from an archive of field recordings. The series is dedicated to helping traditional healers around the world tell their stories.

VOLUME 1
Gary Holy Bull: Lakota Yuwipi Man

VOLUME 2
Ikuko Osumi, Sensei: Japanese Master of Seiki Jutsu

VOLUME 3
Kalahari Bushmen Healers

VOLUME 4
Guarani Shamans of the Forest

VOLUME 5
Vusamazulu Credo Mutwa: Zulu High Sanusi

VOLUME 6
Walking Thunder: Diné Medicine Woman

VOLUMES IN PREPARATION

Shakers of St. Vincent

Brazilian Hands of Faith

Balians: Traditional Healers of Bali

It is Walking Thunder's request that in keeping with her traditional way, Diné is used in place of Navajo in this book.

Notes in the margin are by the editor.

10　The Navajo Nation

Images from the collection of
the Museum of New Mexico

12　Diné Sacred Land

24　The Diné

44　Diné Ceremonials

52　Diné Sandpainting

Walking Thunder of Two Grey Hills　64

Early Memories of Traditional Medicine　66

Finding My Voice　68

Learning from the Elders　72

Sticks, Pollen, and Horny Toads　77

Being Tested　82

David Peters　87

Afterword 165

References 172

Being a Medicine Woman 148

My Teacher Speaks, He Who Walks Away 157

92 The Medicine Way

100 Tough Lessons

104 Native American Church

109 Prayer

110 Mother Earth and the Four Directions

112 Other Medicine People

115 Challenges of Life

121 Taking the Evil Out

122 Medicine Traditions and Crystal Visions

124 Holy Wind and Lightning

126 Sandpainting

140 The Difference Between Commercial
and Ceremonial Sandpaintings

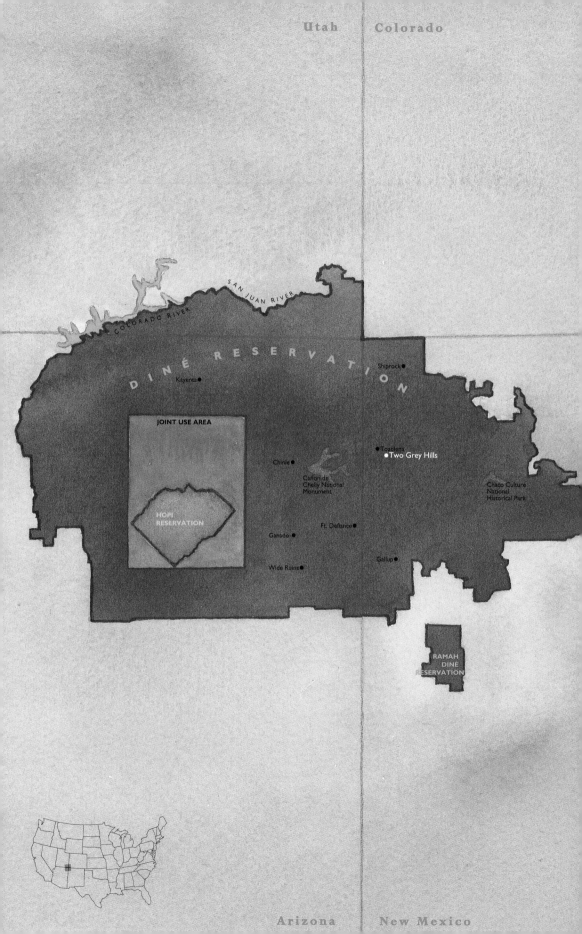

Utah   Colorado

COLORADO RIVER

SAN JUAN RIVER

DINÉ RESERVATION

Shiprock●

Kayenta●

JOINT USE AREA

Chinle●

●Toadlena
●Two Grey Hills

Cañon de
Chelly National
Monument

Chaco Culture
National
Historical Park

HOPI
RESERVATION

Ft. Defiance●

Ganado●

Gallup●

Wide Ruins●

RAMAH
DINÉ
RESERVATION

Arizona   New Mexico

The Navajo Nation

Diné

PHOTOGRAPHER J. R. WILLIS
DINÉ MAN AT CAÑON DE CHELLY RUINS, ARIZONA, undated
NEGATIVE 90519

My nation, the Navajo Nation, is located in the southwestern United States, with land stretching from the northeast corner of Arizona into Utah and New Mexico. It is the largest reservation in the United States. We call ourselves Diné, meaning "the People." I was born on May 8, 1951, in the old hospital at Shiprock, New Mexico. A black nurse looked at my black hair and called me, Juanita. That name stuck with me ever since. On my mother's side, my clan name is Hashtł'ishnii, referring to the Mud People, those who came back with muddy water during the time of origin. I have never known who my father was so I cannot say anything about his side. I grew up in the Two Grey Hills area where a respected man in our community named me Walking Thunder because the name fit my personality and how the people see me. You can call me by my medicine name, Walking Thunder. Welcome to our sacred land.

PHOTOGRAPHER TIMOTHY H. O'SULLIVAN
WHITE HOUSE RUINS, CAÑON DE CHELLY, ARIZONA, 1873
NEGATIVE 146756

PHOTOGRAPHER BEN WITTICK

WINDOW IN THE HAYSTACKS NEAR FORT DEFIANCE, ARIZONA, 1898

NEGATIVE 15554

PHOTOGRAPHER BEN WITTICK

MUMMY CAVE RUINS, CAÑON DE CHELLY, ARIZONA, undated

NEGATIVE 149217

A Prehistoric Fort, Bear Cañon, (Cañon de Chelly) Arizona

Ben Wittick photo

PHOTOGRAPHER Ben Wittick

BEAR CAÑON, CAÑON DE CHELLY, ARIZONA, c. 1900

NEGATIVE 15473

15

PHOTOGRAPHER UNKNOWN
CAÑON DE CHELLY, ARIZONA, undated
NEGATIVE 68802

PHOTOGRAPHER UNKNOWN
CAÑON DE CHELLY, ARIZONA, undated
NEGATIVE 6168

PHOTOGRAPHED BY EL TOVAR STUDIO

MONUMENT VALLEY, ARIZONA, AERIAL VIEWS, undated

NEGATIVES 53438 & 53436 (OPPOSITE)

PHOTOGRAPHER RALPH H. ANDERSON

SPIDER ROCK, CAÑON DE CHELLY, ARIZONA, AUGUST 24, 1940

NEGATIVE 129394

PHOTOGRAPHER HAROLD D. WALTER

CLEOPATRA'S NEEDLE, TODILTO PARK, NEW MEXICO, undated

NEGATIVE 128740

PHOTOGRAPHER WILLIAM PENNINGTON

THE SHIPROCK, NEW MEXICO, undated

NEGATIVE 89512

W e stand on the footprints of our elders. Here are some of our ancestors who walked the beauty way before me. They carried the cultural wisdom and made it possible for us to carry on our traditions today. We honor them through this remembrance.

PHOTOGRAPHER BEN WITTICK

ANSELINA, DINÉ WOMAN, c. 1885

NEGATIVE 15722

PHOTOGRAPHER BEN WITTICK

OLD WASHIE, DINÉ WOMAN, c. 1885

NEGATIVE 16334

PHOTOGRAPHER **BEN WITTICK**

PACHIE, DINÉ WOMAN, c. 1885

NEGATIVE 15946

PHOTOGRAPHER: BEN WITTICK

NINA, WITH CHILD, c. 1885

NEGATIVE 15932

PHOTOGRAPHER KARL MOON

THE WOLF, c. 1906

NEGATIVE 70413

PHOTOGRAPHER GUY C. CROSS

HOSHKEY YAZHIE, DINÉ MEDICINE MAN AND WAR CHIEF, c. 1918

NEGATIVE 119173

PHOTOGRAPHER PENNINGTON STUDIO

BE-ZHOSIE, CALLED THE "MILITANT MEDICINE MAN" AND
LEADER OF THE BEAUTIFUL MOUNTAIN REBELLION, c. 1913

NEGATIVE 89508

DINÉ SUMMER HOUSE, MONUMENT VALLEY, undated

PHOTOGRAPHER T. HARMON PARKHURST

IRENE WILLIE ADEKY, c. 1935

NEGATIVE 3213

DINÉ WOMEN, c. 1935

PHOTOGRAPHER **T. HARMON PARKHURST**

NEGATIVE 3225

PHOTOGRAPHER **T. HARMON PARKHURST**

DINÉ ENCAMPMENT AT LAGUNA PUEBLO, c. 1935

NEGATIVES (CLOCKWISE) 43495, 3211, 66686, AND 3182

PHOTOGRAPHER **PAUL A. WILSON**

FAMILY IN FRONT OF HOGAN NEAR GALLUP, NEW MEXICO, undated

NEGATIVE 86763

PHOTOGRAPHER RALPH H. ANDERSON

PRICE DAUGHTER AND CHILD, CHINLE, ARIZONA, AUGUST 25, 1940

NEGATIVE 130145

PHOTOGRAPHER RALPH H. ANDERSON

NAMBE BEGAY AT CAÑON DE CHELLY, ARIZONA, AUGUST 24, 1940

NEGATIVE 129448

DAISY TAUGEL CHEE, DINÉ WEAVER, TOADLENA, AUGUST 5, 1958

Ceremonial life is important to my people. We have always danced in a sacred way to bring forth the powers of the Holy People. Here are some traditional ceremonials conducted by our ancestral elders. Please look at them with respect.

In the Yeibichai or Nightway Ceremonial, references are made to special holy people called the Yei. The Yeibichai dancers attempt to summon the powers of the Holy People through aligning themselves with mythological narratives enacted in the songs and dances.

PHOTOGRAPHER EDWARD S. CURTIS
YEIBECHAI CEREMONY, undated
NEGATIVE 143873

PHOTOGRAPHER BORTELL
YEIBECHAI CEREMONY, c. 1919
NEGATIVE 91045

PHOTOGRAPHER MULLARKY

YEIBECHAI DANCERS, undated

NEGATIVE 47917

PHOTOGRAPHER HAROLD KELLOGG

YEIBECHAI SINGERS, GALLUP, NEW MEXICO, 1940

NEGATIVE 77523

PHOTOGRAPHER WYATT DAVIS

DINÉ FEATHER DANCE, c. 1945

NEGATIVE 90751

PHOTOGRAPHER MULLARKY

48   FIRE DANCE, GALLUP, NEW MEXICO, undated

NEGATIVE 74866

PHOTOGRAPHER MULLARKY

FEATHER DANCE, GALLUP, NEW MEXICO, undated

NEGATIVE 74871

PHOTOGRAPHER BEN WITTICK

DINÉ SQUAW DANCE, 1901

NEGATIVE 37683

PHOTOGRAPHER T. HARMON PARKHURST

DINÉ SQUAW DANCE, c. 1935

NEGATIVE 3038

PHOTOGRAPHER SALLIE WAGNER

50   MARY TODDY'S KINAALDÁ, WIDE RUINS, ARIZONA, 1940

NEGATIVE 3009, 3012 & 3013 [CHECK #s]

A Kinaaldá is a two-night
ceremony for a woman's
puberty rite.

PHOTOGRAPHER: SALLIE WAGNER
ROSE MARTIN'S KINAALDÁ, WIDE RUINS, ARIZONA, 1946
NEGATIVE 3027

51

L ater I will explain how I learned to make sandpaintings. We use them for teaching about the Creation Story as well as for medicine that heals. We also make them as works of art that we sell to others. That helps keep us alive. This is an old traditon and these photographs show our elders practicing this holy way. What you are looking at is very sacred so please be reverent with it.

Navajo Sand Painting

PHOTOGRAPHER J.R. WILLIS

DINÉ SANDPAINTING, 1922

NEGATIVE 45164

PHOTOGRAPHER UNKNOWN

DINÉ SANDPAINTING, 1922

NEGATIVE 3035

PHOTOGRAPHED BY CROSS STUDIO

DINÉ SANDPAINTING, INDIAN FAIR, SANTA FE, NEW MEXICO, c. 1925

NEGATIVE 1497

PHOTOGRAPHER T. HARMON PARKHURST

DINÉ SANDPAINTERS, c. 1925

NEGATIVES 8721 & 8718 (OPPOSITE)

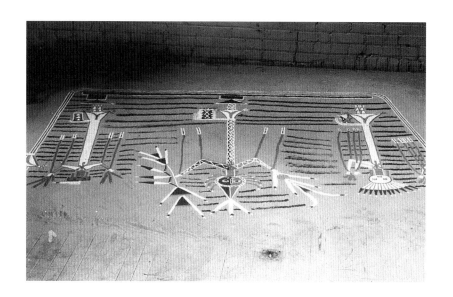

PHOTOGRAPHER UNKNOWN

FRINGE MOUTH TRINITY (PART OF NIGHTWAY),
INDIAN FAIR, SANTA FE, NEW MEXICO, 1926

NEGATIVE 145796

PHOTOGRAPHED BY SAN JUAN STUDIOS

DINÉ SANDPAINTING, undated

NEGATIVE 3039

56

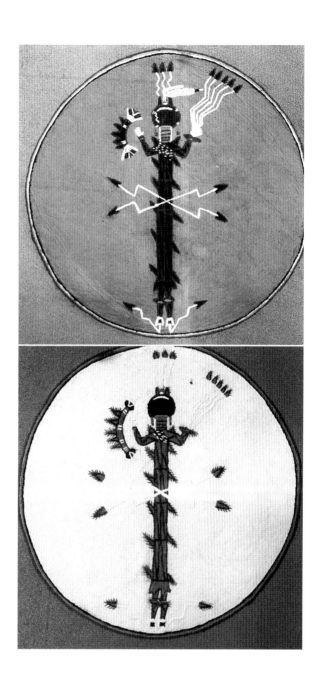

PHOTOGRAPHER UNKNOWN

DINÉ SANDPAINTINGS, undated

NEGATIVES 36418 & 36417

The legendary Hosteen Klah (1867–1937), also called Lefthanded, was one of the most famous medicine men of the twentieth century. He was from the Two Grey Hills area where Walking Thunder lives. Klah, a highly respected weaver, wove sacred sandpaintings and allowed his stories, chants, and rituals to be recorded so that his knowledge would be preserved. With Mary Wheelwright, he founded the hogan-shaped Museum of Navajo Ceremonial Art in Santa Fe, New Mexico (now called the Wheelwright Museum). His teachers had been the informants for Washington Matthews, the first person to write about Diné sandpaintings in 1884.

PHOTOGRAPHER **T. HARMON PARKHURST**

HASTEEN KLAH, DINÉ MEDICINE MAN, c. 1935

NEGATIVE 4330

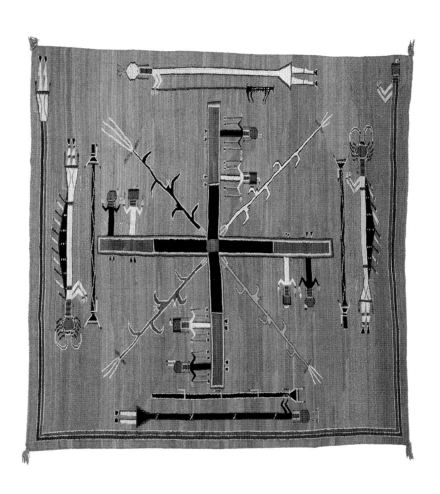

HASTEEN KLAH AND GLADYS MANUELITO (MRS. SAM)

WHIRLING LOGS, OR TSIL'OL-NI, OF THE NIGHTWAY CEREMONY,
WOVEN SANDPAINTING, c.1930s

66½ × 67½ INCHES

PRIVATE COLLECTION

59

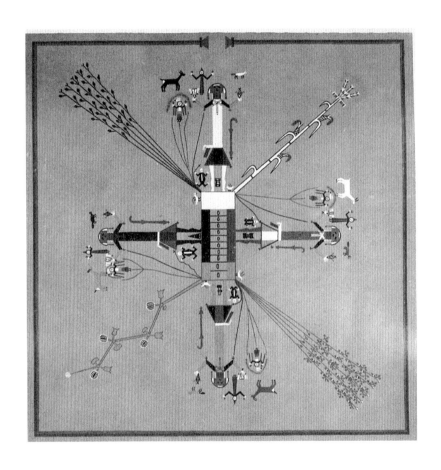

ARTIST FRED STEVENS, 1969

PHOTOGRAPHER ARTHUR TAYLOR

SANDPAINTING FROM THE BEAUTYWAY—NAVAJO EMERGENCE MYTH

NEGATIVE 71137

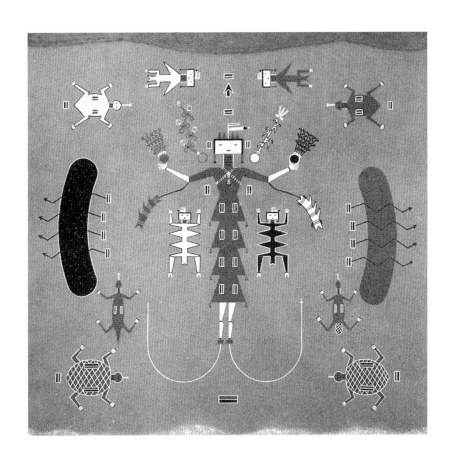

ARTIST FRED STEVENS, 1969
PHOTOGRAPHER UNKNOWN
NEGATIVE 71139

NAVAJO EMERGENCE MYTH, undated

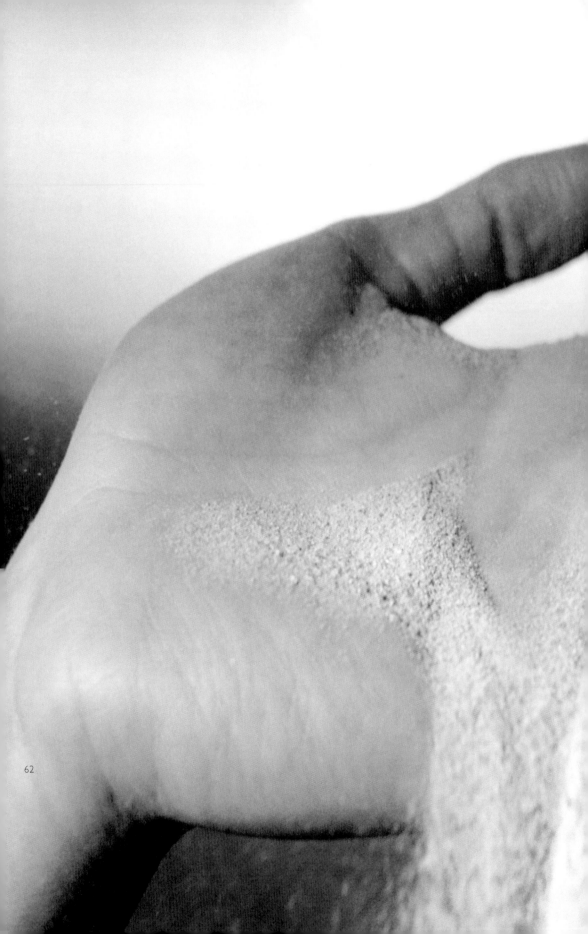

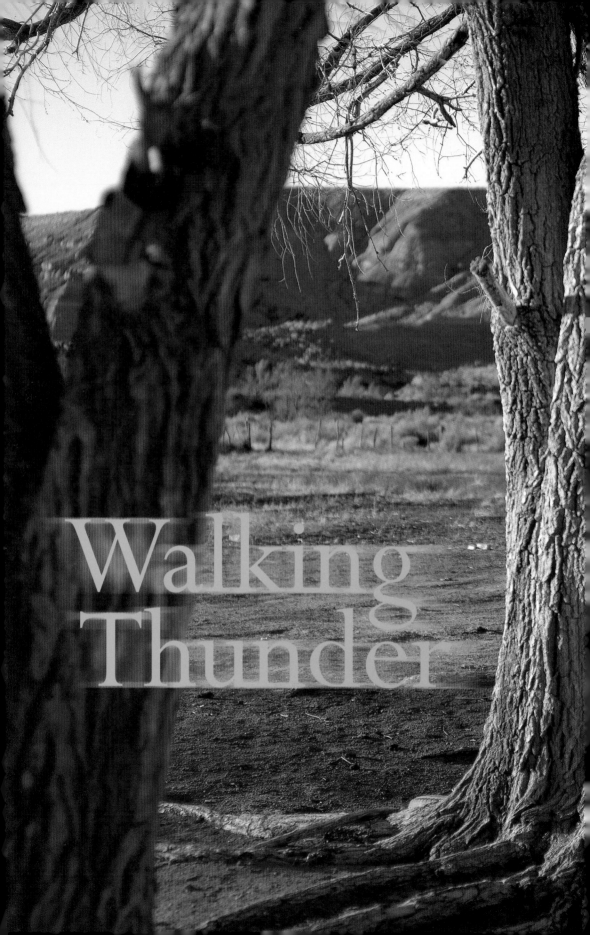

Walking
Thunder

Early Memories of Traditional Medicine

After washing her hands, she sent all the children out and told them to make no noise outside. Next she sprinkled her hand with corn pollen and held it out before her, flexed at the elbow and with the palm up. She sat that way for some time; then the hand began to shake. Her eyes were closed. The hand shook more and more, and felt over the patient. When she had finished, she was breathing hard as if she had been running.

Leighton and Leighton, *Gregorio the Hand-Trembler: A Psychological Personality Study of a Navaho Indian,* 1949, p.158. Reprinted courtesy of the Peabody Museum of Archaeology and Ethnology, Harvard University.

HAND TREMBLING
is one of the major modes of diagnosing illness for the Diné. One becomes a hand trembler when they are spontaneously seized by the uncontrollable trembling and shaking of their right arm (and sometimes their whole body). This is seen as a sign that the person is possessed by the spirit of the Gila Monster. Then a ceremony must be performed so that the trembling is transformed into a manageable experience used to diagnose illnesses. Hand trembling is also used to locate lost objects, identify witches, and to find an enemy.

A Diné medicine person may be a *hand-trembler* and use their hands for healing, or they may limit their practice to dispersing herbs, or to chanting or singing the sacred prayers and songs. The singers who preside over major ceremonials are called *hataáli*. A ceremonial or a performance refers to a complex system of rites and ceremonies typically performed over two to ten days.

HOGAN A traditional Diné shelter—the most common version today is the female hogan—a six-sided dwelling made of logs, with a doorway facing east and a smoke hole in the center of the roof. Traditionally, the hogan is thought to be a microcosmic reflection of the universe.

CEREMONIES Also called ceremonials or performances.

WITCHCRAFT is believed to be widespread among the Diné. Witches or *chindi* are called "skinwalkers" because they go about at night clothed in the skin of a coyote or wolf. The Diné believe that skinwalkers can turn themselves into other creatures and cause illness or death to their enemies.

I remember when I was about six, one of my relatives became sick. She talked about going to a *trembling hands* person. That's my first memory of traditional medicine. We were eating tortillas with melted grease when my family talked about getting her help. I left the house and when I returned later, I saw a medicine man singing over my relative in a ceremony. I came in and he told me not to touch her food. "She's going to be treated as a holy person so please don't ask any questions." But I kept looking at the food. There was a rib as well as peaches and others foods specially made for her. It all looked delicious and I wanted to eat it, but I didn't touch it. They finally told me to stop looking at it.

When I settled down, they did a performance on her. She was sitting up and they painted her body. They took off her blouse but left on her skirt. Then the medicine man smeared stuff on her body. All the while he sang with great intensity. I sat staring at her until they told me to leave. I couldn't see clearly the design they had put on her body. They warned me not to look at it because it would make me blind in the future. That's why I left the ceremony.

Years later, when I was about eight, another ceremony took place. For the performance a small hogan was prepared. My stepfather, who didn't want me to attend, slapped me in the back when I walked into the hogan. He told me that I didn't belong there. I left but immediately crawled back inside and hid behind people who were sitting on the ground. They quietly shuffled their bodies to keep me hidden from my stepfather. As I sat there, I heard people discuss how difficult the situation was and the certain way the patient should stand. Then a medicine man jumped up and declared that they weren't conducting the right ceremony.

Finally they discussed how the sick woman sitting in front of them was no longer in this world. She was very sick and had come to my mom's house for the ceremony because people didn't want any witches to find out what was going on. At the time there was a skinwalker causing a lot of trouble, so ceremonies were hidden for protection. Many medicine men from different areas came for that ceremony. I was curious so I crawled in and listened to their discussions. They talked about how to *backfire* the situation in order to save the woman. My mother said that the woman's body was choosing to die. She was also concerned about witches and said she didn't want to deal with any witchcraft.

It was decided that a particular medicine man would perform a ceremony to help her die. That was when I started to suspect witchcraft was going around. I asked my mom, "Did that medicine man put her away?" Everybody shushed me about it. That's the only time I ever witnessed a performance like that. I kept asking why they put that lady to death and they answered, "She chose it."

I don't know what was in the small pouch they used, but I know they used it to do something to her. I also believe that it was her choice. Her husband didn't want it to happen, but in respect to her intentions, he okayed it. Everybody was respectful of the outcome and the lady went home and died four or five days later.

My very first experience of seeing a skinwalker was when I was ten. I was in the house one evening and heard a door squeak. I figured it must be a cat or dog. I opened the door and saw this huge monster. It scared the hell out of me. It had brown hair and a black face. He also had pouches. This thing almost knocked me out right there. That was my first sight of a skinwalker. After that, I began seeing many of them. There are different kinds of skinwalkers with various shapes and sizes. They can fly, jump, and move fast. Now, I can smell and hear them. I can even feel them. I'm that kind of person. We believe that if you catch a skinwalker and reveal its identity, it will die in three days.

Finding My Voice

After my first ceremony, I started asking a lot of questions about traditional medicine. Why this? Why that? I deeply wondered about what happened when certain practices took place. I even tested things myself. Sometimes I went into the fire to find out things. Sometimes you have to experience things firsthand in order to find out if it's true or not.

For example, when I was about 12 or 13, the community held a performance on my aunt and I decided to test what was going on. I asked why they said and did certain things. For this performance, they were making all kinds of dolls. Without thinking, I automatically took one of the dolls and broke it in half. I thought that a doll was just a material thing that had no power. Although I had been told that the doll was supposed to be a holy person, I went ahead and broke the doll in half. I also broke a whistle and smashed the arrows that came with it. I didn't stop with that. I went on to examine the yucca soup and threw it out. The medicine man said to me, "Since you did these things, something is going to happen to you."

I didn't believe him. I shouted, "Nothing's going to happen to me!" But within two weeks, I became very sick. I couldn't move. When I tried to walk, I just keeled over. People thought I was crazy. During that time I wanted to murder my stepfather and almost did it. I had discovered a mean streak in my body. I ached for worse things to happen and my body felt like it wanted to hurt something. I was told that I was sick, handicapped, retarded, and crazy. Everyone rejected me. That's how I stepped into the fire.

My mom took me to a medicine man and asked what was going on because I was not myself. I drooled and twitched a lot. All the hurt around me made me angrier and angrier and I wanted to do away with somebody. The medicine man did a performance to find out what was happening to me.

He conducted a Talking Back Ceremony where you examine your past and talk back to it. He dressed me up as a bear symbol and painted my face black. He placed many things around my waist and herbs around my body. While he did this, he told me things. He put a band around my head and blew a lot of whistles around me. When he blew those whistles, I felt a wound opening on the top of my head. I felt him take something out of my head with his mouth. He growled, pulled it out, and spit it into the fire. The flames immediately jumped in a frightening way.

What he destroyed was a curse. I learned that my aunt got sick because people had witched her. Those little dolls they made for the ceremony were actually the images of sickness that they put in her. Although they said the doll was a holy person, it was actually a curse.

Symbol for a Talking
Back Ceremony

The medicine man went on to tell me, "For some reason you didn't like the dolls. You automatically destroyed it and that's what got you. Now we know that you're not on the bad side." He explained that there are good medicine people as well as bad medicine people. "Because of this," he added, "you should never trust anybody. Trust only yourself. You have no friends and you have no one you can truly rely on. You are your own friend. And your mind and your breath are yours."

He said many more things before he let me out of the hogan. Going home, I fought for my voice. If he hadn't done those things for me I'd probably have died a long time ago. I had been cursed because I destroyed that doll and smashed those arrows. Instead, the medicine man helped me regain my life and gave me a Warrior's Shield.

At my ceremony the medicine man said, "Now you can start visioning the future. You'll be surprised and you won't believe what's going to happen to you. Also, you're going to have two minds about these things, but in the end you'll get it." That's what he told me, and it was true. He finished by saying, "I will never see you again."

I wondered why he had said that, but sure enough I never saw him again because he died soon after. While he was alive, my family had gifted him with sacred things. We had given him two Navajo baskets full of corn pollen. With those gifts, my mother had begged for my life.

Although we sometimes disagree, when I think back to what my mom did, when it comes to traditions, I know she's on my side. In the details of everyday life, she's often against me, but in our traditional ways, she would never say anything that would harm me.

All you can do is pray for a person who is very sick. Sometimes they get well, but sometimes you can't get them well. You always have to leave things to the Creator. When I destroyed that doll, it was inevitable that something was going to happen to me. The medicine man, who helped me explained how I could overcome it, but he advised me to be careful if I decided to learn how to *backfire* (i.e. reverse) things. He explained that a medicine person had to choose whether they would backfire in a good or bad way. My husband, David, learned the positive way of backfiring. He was good at backfiring things. For example, if a judge or a policeman or enemies came against you, he could twist

Inset: Walking Thunder and her mother.

WARRIOR SHIELD
Believed to be brought about by performing a Warrior Prayer. This prayer helps you to not hesitate in doing the things you want to accomplish. It strengthens you against evil and protects you from things said against you. The Warrior Prayer fights for you. It makes you a shield and makes you strong.

everything around in his prayers and backfire it. Then things turned out with a good outcome. He could turn things around and win. It's a powerful thing to work with and he didn't use it in a mean way, but he used it to win or to get what he wanted. I remember a woman who lost her driver's license because of a DWI and the policeman was ready to testify that she was guilty. My husband performed a ceremony and switched the situation around thereby freeing the accused. My husband sincerely asked the Creator to give the person another chance. Then he made her smoke a sacred tobacco and pray on her own.

Learning from the Elders

David's grandpa was the best medicine man around and all his uncles were also medicine men. His side of the family was all medicine people, going way back. The person they learned it from was called Wind Singing Man. That's who my relatives learned it from and they passed it down. I learned from many medicine people. Sometimes I saw a medicine person in my dreams and then I went to find them.

Also, when I was young I would run up to any elder medicine person and start asking them questions. My sister was ashamed of me for doing that. She would say, "Why do you ask all those questions?" It seemed obvious to me—for me to find out. In these ways I learned our traditional Creation Story. I was also taught sandpainting and what to do in traditional performances. I now do these things in the correct traditional way. Some people add their own stuff and do it their own way, but I do it the traditional way. Among the traditionals, we support others who do it the right way. If someone starts doing it their own way, we don't say anything, we just walk away. It's not wise to criticize another medicine person. They might be practicing witchery. You never know what you are up against. You never question; you just walk out. That's what I was taught.

One of the beliefs we, the Diné, have in our healing tradition is that you have to mean it when you help a person. When I was a young girl, there were many medicine men. Also, many people did the

Traditional Sandpainting

From top to bottom:
Begin the composition.
Stay focused.
Erase painting at end of ceremony.
Mix all the sand.
Pick up the sacred sand.
Return the sand to Mother Earth.

trembling hands and there were many vision makers.

However, there weren't as many medicine women. I remember a few ladies around our area who were medicine women, but they did hand trembling or charcoal visioning. I remember one who was called White Shell Dawn Lady. She was very tiny and she used to give advice to the councilmen. She gave advice to other medicine men when they got into problems. She was there for them and I used to envy her.

Then there was another lady, called Singing Woman from the South, who used to perform in the Native American Church. I admired her. I liked her teaching, her talks, and her jokes. She was my main aunt. Two weeks before she died, she realized how much I admired her and said, "You should have talked to me before, I would have taught you how to bring the eagle to the ground." She could call an eagle down from the sky and pluck out his feathers while the eagle sat on her. She had that kind of a gift. I admired her because she could call an eagle down.

In the last two weeks of her life, Singing Woman from the South was sick in the hospital at Gallup. We went to visit her. When we got there, I walked right up to her, looked at her and said, "You're a medicine woman. Why are you just letting yourself die?" She looked at me and told the other people to leave the room. She told me about eagle feathers—how to carry them, take care of them, their purpose—all in great detail. She kept asking me if I was remembering what she was telling me and kept questioning me to make sure that I was remembering. "Do you know which side to use? Do you know which area?" We repeated this many times until she was satisfied. She taught me the four ways of the eagle feather. At the time, I thought all the ways were the same. During her last days, I asked Singing Woman from the South how she was able to call the eagle down from the sky. She said that even if she gave me one of her songs she uses to call the eagle, I wouldn't be able to do it on my own. "You have to learn to control animals and to control a lot of things. Prayer alone won't work. But if you want to learn I can teach you. However, you have to sacrifice somebody in order to receive this knowledge. You must sacrifice someone you really, truly love, not someone who you hate. It must be a person who is close to your heart." But, I wasn't willing to

VISION MAKERS AND VISIONING
In the Diné tradition, vision makers are diagnosticians who gaze at crystals, specially prepared smoke, or the evening stars. Charcoal visioning refers to visions precipitated by staring at burning coals.

do that. That was bad. I chose to stick with the good ways.

Many years after Singing Woman from the South died, I thought about what she had said about the four ways of the eagle feather. That's when it all started to make sense to me. That was one of the ways how I became a medicine woman.

One of my gifts is asking too many questions, because this brings me knowledge. On the other hand, the holy people sometimes say, "If she really wants to know, let's give it to her directly from the holy side." I'm grateful to have all the ways of receiving sacred knowledge. I have no intention of giving up. It's going to be with me for the rest of my life, for as long as I live. This is what I tell my kids, but I also tell them that I'm a living person. I will do something wrong and I will not be perfect. Nevertheless, I will still be a medicine woman. That's the way I put it.

MAXINE WILSON, MEDICINE WOMAN: I still perform some of the medicine ways. I sing and give traditional prayers, as my father and grandfather taught me to do. They learned from the medicine men who came down from the Long Walk.

I work on people with mixed up minds—people who go to prison and people who have family problems. Most of all, I perform Purity Rites for young girls, the Warrior Prayer, and the Walk in Beauty Ceremonial. When we perform those ceremonies, the patient washes with yucca in the morning, dries off with corn, and then we do the prayers. Every once in a while I do the trembling hands.

I want Walking Thunder to keep doing medicine work for people. She needs to keep helping. I hope that she keeps her head up and doesn't let anyone put her down. With the knowledge and courage she has within herself, nothing should go wrong for her.

MAE K. JAMES, MEDICINE WOMAN: I'm the sister of Maxine. I still perform the medicine way, but my children think I'm too old to continue that work. I know how to use the Waterway to

THE "LONG WALK"
The Anglo-American effort in 1864 to "subdue" the Diné. Kit Carson killed, captured, imprisoned, and then forced thousands of Diné to walk 300 miles from the reservation around Canyon de Chelly to Fort Sumner, on the Pecos River in south-eastern New Mexico.

reawaken someone hurt from falling off a horse, hurt in a car accident or someone in a coma. Within my lifetime I have brought back 15 people from a coma.

When I was young, I wanted to learn all the medicine ways of the medicine men, but some men told me not to do it. I went ahead and did it anyway. I aimed for what I believed in and that's how I learned the medicine way. My father was a powerful man in the Windway. People sometimes thought that he was dirty, but that was because every time he ate meat he put grease on his shoes, body, and hair. The grease was his shield. He could bring the wind into a person.

WINDWAY
A ceremonial used for diseases brought about by "wind infection" (such as heart and lung problems), "snake infection" (stomach trouble), and "cactus infection" (body itching and eye trouble).

WALKING THUNDER: Maxine Wilson was married to my uncle, my mother's brother. I remember going to my uncle's house a lot and it was the only place where I was given meat to eat. I remember seeing Maxine and her husband holding hands and walking around. They were very much in love. I just looked at them and wondered what they were doing. Now I understand what they were doing.

The medicine woman who inspired me the most when I was young was Singing Woman from the South. She is no longer alive. The first time I ever saw her was at a peyote meeting. She had the loudest voice and she made me want to sing like her. The next time I saw her, she was a Ropewoman. I told myself that I wanted to be like her. She was the one who could sing the eagle down. She lived to be 108.

When I was young, I went to many traditional ceremonies. I went to both evil and good practitioners. Although they were real bad about witchery at that time, they used to visit one another. I found I learned something from everyone.

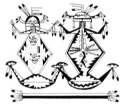

Symbol for Singing Woman from the South

Sticks, Pollen, and Horny Toads

When I was a child, kids my size used to ask me, "Since you're always in the Navajo traditional way, do you think you can do something to help us get over this sickness?" I would say yes and then go break off a stem from one of Mother Earth's plants and start singing. I would sing away and say a prayer, pick up some rocks or another stick and hold them while praying. I would pray in this way for my childhood friends. At the end I would make a big joke about it. I would shout, "Now you're better!" Then I would pull their ears or pull their nose. They'd start laughing. I would say, "If you're laughing, you're going to get well." That was one thing I used to say to the little kids who came to me when they were sick. Or I would just tickle them and say, "You'll be okay."

Even then, as a child, I knew that a stick was a root of life. It can come out good or it can come out bad. I remember one dream that I had as a young girl. In the dream I was in a fog picking up sticks. After the dream I started picking up sticks for my childhood ceremonies. The dreams gave me an education. They told me things, made me wonder, and helped me understand.

Once, when I was in boarding school, our dorm attendant asked me, "What are you going to do with all those sticks and rocks?" I replied, "We're going to build something out of them." She said, "You can't build anything with those sticks and rocks." I responded by going to my friends and having them help me make things. Some sticks became an automobile, while others became tools, trees, and houses. So the sticks in my dreams were about educating, helping, and moving others.

Every time I see a stick I think about it. I believe that if you carelessly break a stick, you may be breaking your own dream. That's what I always say. That's why I tell my kids to not break sticks. The stick in my dream was a life-teaching root. The rocks in my dreams were the same. The heart of rock teaching is found in the designs of the rocks. If you look carefully at a rock and focus on it, it may tell you the life story of the world. It is because rocks hold the stories of the world. That's how they hold earth's wisdom.

Growing up, I picked up rocks and sticks, learning from each one. If I ever needed help, I just picked up a rock or a stick and said a prayer. To me they were sacred. Sometimes today, people ask me why I have so many rocks inside my house along the walls. I tell them that rocks are my education. Then they ask me why I have rocks inside my house since there are so many other rocks out in the world. They don't understand.

My little girl, Nicole, is the same way. She'll bring rocks home and she'll look at them. However, she doesn't keep them. She puts them back where they were. She treats them like a horny toad. If you pick up a horny toad and play with it, you must put it back where it was found. If you don't put it back, you cut off his trail and you cut off your mind. That's what we say about horny toads.

Symbol for the Pollen Way

Pollen As a little girl, my mom taught me the sacred ways of pollen. She'd take off the pollen and put it into a basket. Then we'd cover it with a cloth and say to the sunshine, "This is not yours. This is mine to heal." I was taught that if you didn't say something like that to the sun, it would eat up all your pollen. I tested it and it happened. To this day, I always say, "This is mine, this is going to be for our healer, that's why I'm taking it, leave it alone." We still cover the pollen with a cloth and let it sit there. My mother sang to the east, asking for the one who heals. She'd set the basket on the floor and sing her pollen song that first talks about one's feet being blessed and then the whole body being blessed. Then she'd go back to the basket to see the corn pollen sitting there like sand. A few hours later we'd check it and the pollen would still be there. Again she would say, "Don't eat my pollen, sun."

My pollen song is different from my mother's. I usually have a gourd that I shake before I sing my song. Once in a while, I'll sing it around the house, but not all the time. The pollen song goes with the birds and the flowers. We get all our songs from our hearts. This is especially true for our healing songs. When you sing the healing way, you have to name all the body parts of a human and then state that they walk in beauty. This has to be done in all directions.

My mom and my grandmother taught me that pollen is used to bless ourselves with beauty. All pollen on Mother Earth, along with the plants

Put your feet
down with pollen.
Put your hands
down with pollen.
Put your head
down with pollen.
Then your feet
are pollen.
Your hands are pollen;
Your body is pollen;
Your mind is pollen;
Your voice is pollen;
The trail is beautiful.
Be still.

Pollen Song recorded by Washington Matthews, 1897

Ordinary pollen is shaken from corn, but the concept is
extended to many other things. Red pollen is the pollen
from cattail rushes, and blue pollen is the ground
petals of larkspur . . . yellow powder that collects on
the surface of water is called water pollen. Animals
may be sprinkled with pollen, and then dusted off to
obtain the peculiar life quality of that animal—snake
pollen for instance, or bird pollen. Animals to be killed
for ceremonial purposes are smothered in pollen to
absorb their life force. The symbol of pollen is
concerned with essence. Pollen is a 'living'
component which can be seen as a haze
or sheen around natural forms.

Donald Sandner
Navajo Symbols of Healing
1979, p. 84

and flowers, is a medicine. If you put all the pollens together for a woman to drink, she will not have any problem having babies. She'll deliver quickly and have no difficulties. When a woman drinks the pollen of medicine earth, she will heal and become a virgin again. That's what we were taught. Pollen is pure and has been used as a medicine for women for a long time. When we perform a Walk in Beauty Ceremony, we use corn pollen. In traditional sandpaintings and singing, we use all of Mother Earth's pollens.

Horny Toad I remember when I was young, a medicine man from Shiprock used to ride a horse all the way to Two Grey Hills. When he came, he'd bring a big black box of candy. They used to let us know when he was coming and we ran over there just to get a piece of candy. When we knew he was on his way, we'd make something for him, like a corn pollen bag or jewelry to trade with him for candy. One time, a day before he came, I spent all day looking for a horny toad. I knew horny toads were sacred to him because he had told me a story about them; how they are made and what they stand for. I didn't let the other kids know about the horny toad. They'd be making pouches, bags, or beads while I sat in one place, meditated, and said, "Where's the horny toad?" A certain place came to mind and sure enough, I found one there. I'd keep it in a glass jar with holes in the lid and give it cornmeal and pollen.

First thing in the morning, I ran down to my uncle's house and the medicine man from Shiprock was there talking away. I said, "I've got something for you." He wanted to see it and he took out the horny toad and started praying and putting pollen on him. After that, he dipped it in some water and announced, "We're going to get rain now." Again, he dipped the horny toad in the water, took it out and put corn pollen on him. He told the story about how a long time ago the lightning put a mark on the horny toad. It challenged him, but he survived and the sacred victory the lightning had was by giving a song to the horny toad that would help heal sick people. He'd talk about it that way. He'd count the spots on the toad and say, "This one is still

Preparing the green medicine to help oxygenate the blood.

young." After telling his stories about horny toads, he put the horny toad against his heart and said, "Whatever sickness I have, you take it away, grandpa." When he put it down, he blessed it and told me to put it back where I got it. He gave me my candy and I ran back to return the horny toad.

Being Tested

When I was learning to be a medicine woman, various medicine men came around to test me. They asked me to make a certain sandpainting and asked me its purpose and what it meant. One night, two medicine men came and drew a big sandpainting and asked me about its symbols. It had arrowheads and lightning. One arrowhead was black and another was turquoise with different designs on it. Some designs didn't belong there in the traditional way. I guess they were testing me. I showed them the ones that weren't supposed to be there. They looked at me and asked how I knew. I answered that it was because in this ceremony lightning is never in the arrow; it's only on the person's body. The lightning represents the movement of the human body. Then they put the rainbow down in the wrong way. In the healing ceremony, it's supposed to be put down straight, not curved; just straight down. They asked me about the rainbow symbol. I told them that the red one was for taking pain into the outside and the turquoise was for bringing back the inner beauty for healing. To heal a person, the red one is supposed to be inside. These were the kind of tests I went through.

They also asked me about herbs. They showed me different herbs and I had to say the name of the herb and what it was good for. I failed on two. One was for whooping cough and the other for sinus headache. I thought the latter one was for some kind of a lung problem. They laughed when I made that mistake. At the time I didn't know that there was a medicine for whooping cough. This medicine smells very strong and makes you sneeze a lot. You sneeze for a while but then that's when the cough stops. Your nose drains for about five minutes and then you forget that you had a cough.

Sacred objects from Walking Thunder's gourd box: Vision Crystal and Warrior Prayer Stick.

Left: pollen
Opposite: *Horse Candy*,
an aphrodisiac for
horse breeding

Below from left to right:
sacred medicine;
sacred tobacco;
medicine for calming
the body; medicine
for making rain

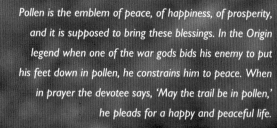

Pollen is the emblem of peace, of happiness, of prosperity, and it is supposed to bring these blessings. In the Origin legend when one of the war gods bids his enemy to put his feet down in pollen, he constrains him to peace. When in prayer the devotee says, 'May the trail be in pollen,' he pleads for a happy and peaceful life.

Washington Matthews, *Navajo Legend*, vol. 5 of "Memoirs of the American Folklore Society," 1897, p. 249

My feet are all sorts of pollen, it shows my way;
My legs are all sorts of pollen, it shows my way;
My body is all sorts of pollen, it shows my way;
My thoughts are all sorts of pollen, it shows my way;
My voice is all sorts of pollen, it shows my way;
My feathers are all sorts of pollen, it shows my way;
I am covered with all sorts of pollen, it shows my way. . .
Behind me, it is beautiful, it shows my way;
Behind me, it is beautiful, it shows my way

from the Creation Story

They also tested me on how long I could sit. We started in the evening and sat still through the night. We sat with a medicine man, The man Who Walks Away, who was doing a crystal vision. He had a big crystal and after he started talking, I became dizzy. He tested me. We talked all day and then he talked all night. The next day, he began to lie down saying he was going to rest his back. He was tempting me but I continued doing my work. At first I did my beadwork. Then I did my sandpainting while he kept on talking. Next, I did my carving and then my spinning. I always made sure I had something to do while he was talking. I concentrated on what I was doing. That's how I passed the test. We stayed up for 36 hours. He was the one who went to sleep. I stayed awake. My husband was chewing and smoking tobacco and then whispered, "He's testing us." I whispered back, "Oh." We just kept doing all those things. After the medicine man left, my bed looked so good and I wanted to jump in, but I didn't. Sure enough, two hours later the medicine man came by the house again when I was cooking. If we had jumped back in bed we would have failed. He popped in and said, "Oh, you're still up?" I said, "Yes, we're still up. Do you want to eat with us?" He came in and ate with us, sat there for a while, and then said, "I'm going now, for sure." We didn't take the chance and waited until the sun went down before we got into bed.

I was also tested to see whether I could find a lost person with my crystal and to see if I could diagnose a sick person with it. A medicine man, who is like a clan brother to me, sent his son-in-law who said his son was sick. The grandson of the medicine man said, "It hurts right there." I looked at him with the crystal and saw that he was not sick. I said, "You're not sick. But you can go outside and shovel my dirt." That brought a smile to the medicine man.

My mom tested me too. She would say, "I lost my wallet and I don't know where it is. Can you find it with your crystal? I've been looking for it for two days. It has $150 in it and I'm really anxious to get some of that money." She did this when I was about 22. I did a crystal vision on her and saw her standing in the woods laughing. That told me that she was faking. To my surprise, the crystal vision also showed me where she was keeping the wallet. I took her straight to the wallet and told her, "It's going to backfire on you if you continue to play jokes on me." If you play with the traditional ways, for money, for example, you'll have problems with money. That's what she did with me. She said she had money but never that much. Ever since then, money has been awkward for her. Even though she did that to me, I still help her. That's never going to change.

David Peters

The first time I met my husband, David, I assumed that he lived far away from me. To my great surprise, he lived only two miles away. This was when I was in school and my teacher told me to take a film projector to the next classroom. When I went into the classroom, I saw him there. I looked at him and he looked at me. It was love at first sight. In our minds it felt right. He told me later that he was thinking, "She's going to be my wife." At the same time, I was thinking, "That's the man I'm going to see without pants." I stared at him for such a long time that the teacher shouted at me to wake up. I just looked at him, put the projector down, and smiled. All his classmates were laughing.

I never had a crush on anyone but him. He was my first love. However, on that day, we didn't talk. We just looked at each other and smiled. He later wrote me a letter putting my name with his last name. That's when I knew for sure that I had him. I was so happy.

He was a nice man and our marriage was very good for 30 years. It was good until the last two years of his life. The doctor told him that he was going to die because of a heart problem. But David never told me. He just said he wanted to enjoy life. His life ended due to heart failure at the Comfort Inn motel. He said he was going to die in style—the room had a big TV and a big bed in it. He just lay down on one side of that bed and died there.

He was a good medicine man. I remember he once gave a performance for two young girls who were twins. He said he was going to do a Warrior Prayer for them. His father wanted to witness it so his dad and I went up there. When we arrived, we found people dressed in traditional full skirts. They had sheep and lambs they were feeding with a bottle. They lived very traditionally. They had no running water or any other modern conveniences. David's job was to say a prayer for these twin girls. I wondered how he was going to do it, and before I knew it, he began to pray. I saw that he went deep inside himself and didn't hear anything around him. He just prayed for the little ones.

After a while, he began talking. At first, I thought he was talking to me, but he was talking to someone else. I didn't know who he saw, but when I asked him afterwards, he said it was a holy person. The holy person blessed those two girls and said that something was going to happen to one of them. David's father knew he was talking to a holy person and so he poured water onto the floor. Then he put pollen on the spilled water for the Holy One present at the ceremony.

After we left, we went to a big yucca plant and David pulled it in four different directions. He stabbed himself with the plant. When I asked him about it, he said it was because he was worried about one of his patients, the little girl. He then started crying. He started bleeding from the yucca and he gave his blood to Mother Earth. His father did the same thing.

Every time a medicine person does a traditional Diné practice, they have to do something to their body if they believe something bad is going to happen to a patient. True medicine people do it. I asked David about it and he just said it's one of the traditional ways. As a natural law, it's a way of communicating with Mother Earth and Father Sky. Because they spill their blood for us, we sometimes must do the same. There's a telephone line between the Creator and us. Everything we medicine people do helps communication take place with the Holy Ones.

I never knew my husband was a medicine man until we were married. We were married at the Bureau of Indian Affairs up in Shiprock. It wasn't a big ceremony. The only witnesses were my sister, my mom, and his father. The BIA bought us a small cake. That's how we got married. Afterwards we went to the highest mountaintop, put our vows together, and said things to each other. Then we used the whistle to bless one another. We also cut ourselves. I still have the scar from that cut on my hand. That's our way of having a traditional marriage.

One night we both dreamt about a medicine pouch and how we were going to make it. I got out of bed and walked around looking for the buckskin to make the pouch. He was also looking for the buckskin at the same time. We didn't know that our son had taken it to the hogan to make a drum out of it. Finally we met in the middle of the room and he asked me what I was looking for. We then realized that we were both looking for the same object to do the same thing with it—to make a medicine pouch from a dream. We knew then that we had experienced the same dream at the same time.

Another time, we had a dream about his mother. We both jumped out of bed together and said, "Mom is dead!" We said it at the same time. We ran to her house and sure enough she was dead. That's the way we dreamed.

On another occasion, we both had the same dream about buying a car. In the dream, after we left the car dealer, we had an accident. We had actually planned on buying a car that day, but changed our minds because of the dream. We didn't buy a car until a whole month later. David said that we needed to have a moon change before buying a car.

My husband believed in the Moonways, the Storyways, the Windways, and The Rainways. He said those were his messengers. For example, after staring at a storm cloud, he announced that a war was coming on very soon. I said, "There's no war. Vietnam is over." He kept looking at the storm and said, "I feel there's going to be a war and there's this one person getting all his feathers up." Sure enough, Desert Storm took place soon after his vision. The storms told him things like that.

We had gone about forty miles when heavy, wind-blown clouds darkened the sky and hard gusts made driving difficult. Suddenly I looked across the mesa to my right and exclaimed, What's that?" Everyone looked that way and Arthur said, "It's a cyclone!" He stopped the car and we watched the black hourglass column as it spun and swayed on a path that would take it across the road about a half-mile in front of us. We were already beginning to feel the side winds sucking in toward the center, when, to our horror, it turned directly toward us. We had all been standing in front of the car watching the progress of the funnel; now I told the girls to hurry and rushed to climb into the car. But not Klah. He started walking slowly toward the whirling mass, which was approaching with the sound of a thousand swarms of bees. Stooping now and then to pick up a pinch of earth or part of a desert plant, he put the accumulation into his mouth even while he was chanting. We could not very well turn around and go away, leaving him to face the tornado alone, and anyway, it was now much too late to make our escape, so we simply sat there—four of the most frightened humans anyone ever knew. Klah continued to walk slowly into the eddying wind, then suddenly held up both hands and spewed the mixture in his mouth directly at the approaching column and raised his voice to a loud chant. The column stood still for a moment and then divided in the center of the hourglass, the upper part rising to be obscured by the low hanging clouds and the lower half spinning away at right angles to its former course like a great upside-down top.

Franc Johnson Newcomb, *Hasteen Klah: Navajo Medicine Man and Sand Painter*, 1964, pp. 198–199.
Inset right: Hasteen Klah and family, undated.
Photographer: Franc Newcomb,
Museum of New Mexico, negative 90757

The
Medicine
Way

The inseparability of spirituality from other
aspects of life is reflected in the fact that there is no word
for 'religion' in Navajo; nahagh (a ceremony is taking place)
is the closest equivalent to this English word.

Trudy Griffin-Pierce, *Earth Is My Mother, Sky Is My Father: Space,
Time, and Astronomy in Navajo Sandpainting*, 1992, p. 29

I worked with my husband in the medicine way. If he was going to perform a ceremony on a teenager or a woman, he asked me to sit with them. If he was going to perform on a man, he would let me sit by his side. He always told me that I was his witness.

You shouldn't work on someone alone. If he didn't have someone with him, he got a stick from the fire and put it between the patient and himself. That's how he performed. Although he was never ashamed, he was very strict about his traditions. He always told you the way things should be. He never beat around the bush. He'd tell you what was going to happen without any qualms.

Of his ceremonies my favorite was his Sunburst Ceremony. He used it for young kids. It uses one of my favorite symbols, which is a sun with a horn. The Sunburst is for a restless person who is too closed in and doesn't want to learn. A person who's hyper all the time and doesn't pay attention to others needs this. The Sunburst is for many young people. It is also used for an adult who doesn't speak up, yet wants people to see that he or she is present.

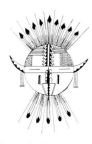

Symbol for The Whirling Logs Ceremony

The Whirling Logs Ceremony is for someone aiming for success. We did this for one of our daughters who wanted to quit college. We wanted her to see the beauty of life in the world and not to quit and give up. He talked to her and I also talked to her. We sat with her and we all cried. Finally we decided to do this ceremony for her and told her to dress in her best clothes and focus on being herself, not someone else. She put on the sacred clothes we wear when we're doing a ceremony. David's father performed the ceremony while David and I made the sandpainting. At the end of the ceremony, the words *enter into beauty* are said. It's like saying you will always walk in beauty. It means that every step we take is more precious than the last. With this understanding, each step I take becomes more and more precious. What we're saying is to be positive with each step. The step you take to get out of bed is the beginning step. Then the second, third, and fourth steps are your four sacred steps. The rest is your sacred walk.

When I was 18, I made a serious commitment to be a medicine woman. That's what I've been doing to this day. My children were good helpers when they were young. When they all lived here with me

Nicole
(daughter)

"Diamond"
(granddaughter)

Jonathan
(son)

Darryle
(son)

Danzee
(son)

Wednesday
(found on the highway on a Wednesday morning)

Walking Thunder's four daughters and their families. From top to bottom: Victoria Peters and Leerolline Burke with daughters Jerrica and Jalaka; June and Dennis Heim, Jr.; Veronica Peters with son, Santana David Smith; Verdella Peters and Ray Joe with daughter, Makayla

Right: Walking Thunder's son, Darryle, with his family. Clockwise from upper left: Darryle, his wife Barbara, Kyle, Darmel, "Diamond," baby Rochelle, Ricardo, and Chavez in front of his Dad.

they would make the medicine and grind the sand for me. They used to get the pouch ready for me in the morning. Now I have to fix everything myself.

When I hold a ceremony, I wear a scarf around my head so my sweat won't fall and mix with the sandpainting. The sandpainting is like a sacred cleanser. You can't dirty it. You also wear the scarf to help keep your mind together. Black is the sacred color I wear. I wear it for the people who have left the earth. I like to wear black with turquoise around me. This is how I perform.

I believe that we pray to one God. I know there's a holy person out there somewhere. I don't talk against the Bible or other ways of worshipping God. All ways to God are good.

I was taught that you should listen to the thunder when you have an important decision to make. Most of our older people look out the window and listen to the thunder when it rains. They wait and listen for their answers. My grandpa used to do that. He used to sit and watch the thunder coming in. You'd hear him say, "That's it. Aah." I don't know what he meant, but he'd say, "Aah." I'd ask him, "What's the matter with you, Grandpa? Are you going crazy the Diné way?" He'd just laugh and go back to listening to the thunder.

When people come to me with their sicknesses and problems, I sometimes have to go to a special place and say a prayer. When you help someone, you must be willing to pray all night and to cry or laugh with them. That's what medicine's about. All that is within your patient must come to you and when you work with them, they are your only concern.

A person who conducts a Trembling Hand Ceremony can tell you what direction you should take your life. For example, they can tell you where you should live. They'll start trembling as they pray or sing about it. They put pollen on their hand to indicate the different directions and put a mark that symbolizes you. They also put a rainbow on the hand and circle the palm all the way around to make it into lightning. They don't use the north because that is where the evil goes. They don't fool around with the north. That's why they only use three directions.

Some of them will tremble lightly while others will shake. I've seen all kinds of trembling. The way their hand moves gives them a diagnosis.

It will tell the healer your sickness, as well as where it comes from. If the healer's hand hits Mother Earth, it means death. If it hits something like a piece of furniture, it means that the sickness will get worse. Sometimes when the healer's hand is very shaky, they can help the patient by passing it over the patient's body.

There are still some powerful hand-tremblers today. Once in a while when I'm trying to help my mom or aunt, I'll go to them. I really can't help my mom in the healing way. Even when she's very sick, I can't help her because I'm her flesh and blood. It will not tell me anything about her sickness. It will not make me feel how she feels inside. I tried it when she was very sick and it didn't do anything. The same thing happened with my aunt, but I have helped her children and grandchildren. I asked a medicine man why I can't understand my mom's sickness and he said the reason was that my mom had rejected me a long time ago. She's still a good mom, though.

Once a black friend of mine got cancer and asked my husband and me for help. We went into the woods and brought her some herbs. Sure enough, the medicine healed her. She didn't even have to go through the surgery recommended for her. She lived and went on to have another child. She told us that the medicine got her horny. We had a good laugh about that. From then on, we decided to use our medicine on people of all colors. The medicine that cured her came from David's father who taught David about the medicine.

Symbol for Replanter for Medicine Herbs

There is a medicine man out there trying to get one of my medicines from me. One day he got sick and his face went crooked. He wanted a certain medicine that I have. We took it to him but he wasn't home and we never had a chance to treat him. I went over to his house three times, but he was never there. I heard that his face is still crooked and he's still looking for his medicine. I know that if I go over there again, the medicine will backfire on me. He has to come to my house and ask for it again.

When my husband's mom was about to die, he saw a bright red/orange light outside our window. He remembered that his uncle had seen the same colored light when his wife was about to die. It's a sign of a death. I, too, have seen that light. I remember getting up at 11 o'clock one night to go to work. When I started the car, everything went bright red/orange around the area. I tried not to believe what was happening, but the next day my husband died. That colored light tells us that someone is going to die.

Tough Lessons

My stepfather abused me. He hit me with chains when I was young. He also chased me with a horse and he hit me with barbed wire. He was an ugly man. I used to say that on the day he died, I was going to dance on his grave and spit on his face. When he finally died, my husband and I went to view his coffin. I was happy he was dead and I was planning to kick his coffin and throw dirt on him. But when I went up to his corpse and looked, I felt sorrow. I didn't want to abuse him or be unkind in any way. I simply turned around and walked away. My husband started to laugh and said, "You got the message."

David told me that he had felt the same way about a particular medicine man a long time ago. The medicine man had performed a ceremony on him when he was a boy. He was hit by a horse so badly that he couldn't urinate. He kept passing out all the time. His father didn't want to take him to the hospital and when he was near death, his father brought in this medicine man to doctor him. The medicine man worked on his butt and made him urinate. But then he did some stuff to him, not in a sexual way, but in an uncomfortable way. My husband hated him and he also wanted to kick his coffin. Years later when he went to the medicine man's funeral, he had a vision of a holy man standing in the room. He then realized that he must stop hating him.

A powerful education takes place inside you when you feel these transformations of attitude and understanding. They can change your life. That's what it did to me. I went deeper into the spiritual path. The difficulties of life can push you in this positive direction. If you allow it, they can push you a little bit forward. After we left my stepfather's coffin, my husband asked me, "Did he teach you?" I simply replied, "Oh." We didn't go to eat or anything. We just went home. And then he said, "Now it's time for you to roll a smoke for all the things you thought about him and for all the things you wanted to do. It's time for you to repent in our Diné way so you'll feel better about yourself. If you don't do it, you will continue to feel that way about others like him and I don't want you to do that." Then he made me roll a smoke and I prayed with the traditional charcoal on the floor. This was one of the things I learned the hard way.

They named me *Walking Thunder*, partly because of my loud laughter. People recognize my laugh. They hear it and say, "Oh, she's here." They also know that when they say something wrong, I'll jump up. Then they say, "She's going to start stirring up trouble." I disagree with things that disturb me, and I talk a lot and laugh a lot. However, I don't show my sadness in front of others. I'm always happy in public. But deep down inside, I have sadness in me. I don't show it unless I'm alone because the medicine man who did a performance on me when I was 12 told me to never show my feelings because others will think I am weak. I think that's the reason I'm this way. But when I'm alone, I allow myself to be sad. If I'm doing a traditional performance and I feel like it, I may bring out my sadness.

My sadness is what makes me fight. It helps me be strong and makes me want to do more rather than less. After my husband died, I blamed everything on the Creator. I even talked against the Creator. But my husband came to me in a dream and told me that I shouldn't feel that way. He told me other things, too, and that's what led me back to practicing the medicine way. People are happy and grateful that I picked it up again. If I didn't, I would not live more than five years. That's the truth. That's what happens. If I don't practice the medicine way, my energy drains away and I open the door for other influences. Other people can't tell you to do this. It has to be your decision.

However, my husband helps me through my dreams by showing me many things. He tells me that he regrets doing some things when he was in this world. He now talks about his past. I also tell him about my dreams and he helps me understand them. He sometimes asks, "Do you want that or do you want this?" He explains that challenges come to me because it's part of the learning process of being a sacred person.

I'm a person for the Creator. There are good and bad practitioners and I'm one of the good ones. Although I don't want to learn the bad way, I know how to fight it. But I have to be careful because it can backfire on me. The Thunder Sandpainting Ceremony was performed on me when I was young. After that ceremony, I didn't feel afraid anymore. It made me feel more positive about life's challenges.

About 12 years ago, we performed a ceremony on a teenager who needed help. She had run away for days and then came back. Her mother didn't understand what was happening to her. As soon as the ceremony started, I looked at the fireplace and began to pray. Immediately, something slapped me on the face. It was a real slap on my face, but I didn't see anyone do it. Others in the room said my face got red on the side where I felt the slap. I thought that maybe I was the only one experiencing this, in my head. I started praying and, again, I was slapped. As I was hit, I looked at the girl and saw her dressed as a skinwalker. The vision came to me like that. When I looked at her again, she was normal. I told my husband who was sitting beside me and he said that the ceremony was going to take all night. He had sensed it when the girl came in because there was a vibration that warned him. The mother and sister, who were also inside the hogan, just said that the girl had been gone for four days. She came back for one day and then left again for another four days. They wondered why she was doing this when their nephew was becoming very sick. Later that night, at around midnight, I saw the claws in her hand. I looked at her with my spiritual sight and saw something white on her hand. I started smelling something evil, but she became a human again.

I left the hogan to wash my face. I was outside washing and I turned and saw her witch spirit standing in front of me. I almost died right there. I fell back and she started shaking something. When I turned again, she had moved to a different place. I went to my husband telling him that I wasn't going to go outside anymore because the girl was outside doing bad things. He said that the girl was sitting inside the whole time I was out. I told him again that she was also outside.

We continued praying over her and sometime in the early morning the girl spoke, "I can't do it." My husband asked her what she couldn't

Skinwalker Story

BILL, WALKING THUNDER'S NEIGHBOR: It was early in the morning, around 2:30 a.m., and I was getting ready for work. I'm a truck driver and left my house to pick up Walking Thunder's son, Daryl, to travel with me. I picked him up and we went down to Thriftway for some coffee. We were driving along Route 666, and at about 3:30 in the morning, something crossed the road that was unlike anything I've ever seen in my life. It was about 50 feet in front of us so we had a good view of it. It was orange and yellow and about four feet high. It was part goat and part mountain lion. It had a goat's tail but no feet or hooves. It just kind of floated and hopped. It was also part human. Underneath the goat's head, you could see another face. The face was pink. It was a skinwalker.

Immediately after seeing this creature, things started to go wrong in my life. My truck kept breaking down. About a week later, I kept seeing coyotes everywhere. The Diné believe that coyotes warn you about evil that surrounds you. So I contacted a medicine man. After the medicine man held a ceremony in my house, my troubles went away. And to my surprise, I unexplainably developed photographic memory that enabled me to make wood carvings. Now I make my living as a carver.

WALKING THUNDER: Bill was an unbeliever before that experience. He used to question us and say, "There's no such thing as a skinwalker." And I'd say, "One of these days, Bill, one of these days." When I found out that Bill had seen a skinwalker, I said, "Bill's going to get a gift back if he does it right and asks the right true medicine man." Sure enough, he came around with his wood carvings one day and that was the gift. Now he has to believe.

do. I kept praying and again she said, "I can't do it." Then I asked her what she couldn't do. "I can't let my nephew die," she said. "I can't let him die. Can you take this away from me?" I asked her what she wanted us to take away and she said, "I was learning how to be a witchcrafter, a skinwalker." I asked her why she would want to do that. She said, "Because I want good things. I only want it to get food and jewelry, sheep, and cows. That's how I wanted to become rich. That's why I wanted to learn it. The man told me to sacrifice a person. Since my nephew is the only person I love and get along with and talk and play with, he had to be sacrificed. That's why he's sick." Her mom got up and asked her daughter, "Why are you doing this? We have enough. We have sheep, horses, cows, and all that stuff." The girl continued and said that she and her teacher had removed a man's corpse from a grave and brought him back to life. They cut him up and used his body in a witch's ritual. "I had to eat his flesh in order to change myself into another animal. That's how I can sit in here but also be outside."

We straightened her out and we got her to pray. All we could do was pray for her. We also fanned her down and cleaned her up, and we made her take some herbs and hoped that she would vomit the bad things she had taken in. The ceremony lasted through two evenings. That girl is still living and walking. She looks normal, but deep down she is no longer focused. We saved her life, but she's still a little bit off in her mind.

Native American Church

Medicine men and women deal with herbs, sandpainting, singing, or chanting. Some of them also deal with witchery and all kinds of hocus pocus on the other side. In addition to medicine people, there are Roadmen. They work with peyote, cedar, sage, smoke, prayers, and songs. Here we eat peyote and concentrate on the cedar in the fire. It requires sitting all night through a meeting where we sing, pray, teach, and talk.

The Native American church has been with me for a long time. The first time I ever tasted peyote was when I was about six. My mom said to come over and take some coffee grounds. I went over and it sure

NATIVE AMERICAN CHURCH: A pan-indigenous organization that uses peyote as a sacrament in ceremonies that are called "peyote meetings." Membership is estimated to be as many as 300,000 among seventy different tribes.

PEYOTE MEETING: Usually performed to cure an illness, it also can be used for giving thanks, receiving blessings, or celebrating a birthday. There are typically four officials who run the meeting: the Roadwoman or Roadman (the main leader), the Chief Drummer (responsible for assembling the drum), the Cedarman (throws ground cedar onto the fire to create a sacred incense), and the Fire Chief (manages the fireplace).

Above: *Native American Church* by Leerolline Burke, 2000

didn't taste like coffee. She was using peyote and prayer for courage to face the difficult things in her life. That evening when she let me eat the peyote medicine, after 10 or 15 minutes, my body began to tingle. People say that's how the medicine starts to work. At the time, I was a hyperactive child and the medicine made me more hyper. I remember going outside and chasing a chicken. After a while, I went to sleep.

I continued to eat the peyote medicine as a child. When I was about nine, I attended a full peyote meeting. I wanted to see how it was, what they say, and what they do. I wanted to witness it myself. My sister and I hid behind some people and observed the meeting. The medicine man talked and afterwards he started the prayers while each person rolled up a smoke. With the smoke, they all started praying. When the medicine came around the third time, I grabbed a bunch of it and swallowed it without chewing. It was green and watery looking. Soon, I started feeling something and then we moved to the front to sit with the others. When the staff came near me, I grabbed it. Someone wanted me to sing. A man was playing the drum. That was the first time I started singing.

Even though I didn't know any songs, a song came to me automatically. I sang pretty well. The medicine man in charge of the meeting told me to come up front. He announced that I was going to be a medicine woman in the future and that I was going to have it all. He knew this because he saw it through my song. He then prayed, cedared me down very well, and gave me four medicines. He turned to my stepfather and said to me, "If he ever hurts you again, you come and tell me." Boy did I feel big and strong. That's when I started standing up for myself. My stepfather was mean. He used to hit me and chased me with a horse. He also beat my mom with a stick. That's the kind of house I lived in.

I remember one vision that changed things for me. As a child, I was often sick. My brother finally paid attention, "Sister, I want you to have this ceremony done on you. I'm tired of you being sick all the time. I want you to get better." I was so sick that I wore a towel on my head. I used to get real hot. A meeting was held for me in the traditional Native American way. The medicine man conducting the meeting said I was visioning things I wasn't supposed to see. I would see a woman in the hospital and know where her pain was located. I would look at her and see an area of her body that was dark. Sometimes I'd see something black around her or I'd see a bug eating her.

I could also smell the sickness and I could smell a person's blood. If a woman had sex the night before, I could smell it. My nose was that good and my ears and eyes were also very good. I learned that all the smells and things I saw made me get sick. That's why they had a peyote meeting. The medicine man gave me a spoonful of medicine every 30 minutes. I was flying high, as you would say in the white man's way. The medicine was really working on me and gave me visions. I told the medicine man that it was getting scary because I started seeing graveyards where people were buried. I saw the bodies lying there and the marks on the coffins. The medicine man said that my sickness had to do with the Ghostway. It involved people who had died. I never found out who made that happen to me and I didn't question it.

When the peyote medicine started doctoring me, I felt puffy. I felt like I was sitting high in the sky. It made me feel the people around me but I could only see their feet. The medicine fixed me up inside and my body hurt from it. I heard my heart beat and my liver move. I heard my insides moving and saw my own fat. I was able to see myself in a true way.

After taking more medicine, my vision focused like a TV set and I could see into my past. I viewed the time when my sister and I butchered and cooked an old, small gray desert lizard. I don't know why we did it, but we didn't eat it. We had mistreated Mother Earth and I learned that that was responsible for the soreness inside me.

Even after the meeting was over and the medicine man went away, the medicine continued to work on me for another week and a half. People came to my house asking for help because they believed I was under the influence of holy spiritual ways. I went and helped them. I prayed and used the sacred things I had been given. From that point on, many patients came to me.

The word got out and more and more people came. I would be awakened around 2 or 4 in the morning with somebody knocking at my door. That's how bad it became. Because of the frustrations, we moved away. We moved from Two Grey Hills in New Mexico to Denver.

GHOSTWAY: sickness caused by witches or ghosts

The Diné believe that sickness and misfortune are the consequence of being out of harmony with the natural world. Inappropriate interaction with natural phenomena, such as wind, thunder, and lightning may cause an imbalance as can the improper contact or mistreatment of animals. Ghosts and witches can also bring about disharmony and illness. Ceremonies and prayers are used to bring a person back to harmony with nature, thereby restoring health and beauty.

Somehow people found out and started coming again. The Diné out there started coming to me. Since I couldn't escape it, we decided to move back to Two Grey Hills again.

I found that if I tried to get away from helping others, I would get sick. That's why I stopped running. Years later, my husband and I decided to face this truth and we asked the Creator to not send too many patients to us because we are not so strong, but that we will help some of His people. That's how we did it. We sat down, had a smoke, and then we sang and prayed about it. We simply told the Creator how we wanted it.

Today when I eat the peyote medicine, I feel the spirits changing me. I see a lot of things. It gives me spiritual focus. I even see things I don't want to see. I can see what every person wants. When the medicine is working on me, I feel like I'm floating. The medicine also helps me see whether there is a skinwalker in the area.

Some medicine people became jealous of me because I had more patients than they did. Other medicine men tried to steal the methods I used to treat my patients. They tried to imitate what I did. What they forget is that when you are performing, it is the holy person in you who is working on a patient. I had to learn to live with these challenges.

Sometimes I'm tired and I don't feel I can help people. I have even tried to hide from my patients. Once, an old lady came for help and I told my family to tell her that I wasn't at home. I crawled under the bed and pretended I wasn't home. I was hiding there and pretty soon I saw the tip of her cane. She lifted up the sheet and saw me under the bed, and demanded that I get out of there and work on her. I didn't know what to say. I just got up and got my medicine pouch. I didn't say a word. She came after me for doing that. After I finished helping her, she started to laugh and make jokes. She finally said, "Don't you ever do that again."

One reason I used to hide was because some people didn't really believe in what I was doing. Their disbelief came back to me and made me sick. Sometimes they wanted to test me and I didn't want to deal with that. I never put a price on my services. I just take what they give me. My grandpa used to say, "Never overcharge people because what you do was given to you as a holy gift." If you're gifted, you're not supposed to ask for money. You have to let the patient decide.

The Big Hogan Vision Years later, I dreamt that I saw the biggest hogan in the world. I saw myself sitting in a corner of this hogan and I was really singing away. A voice in the vision said to me, "You need to be sitting over here." Immediately I flew to that corner and thought, "This is a dream. It's not real life." When I sat in that place, I became sick. The voice then said, "We need to put her back." They brought out a big mattress and sat me on it. I then threw up and thought that I had died. However, I found that I could now see through things. I could see through walls and through hogans. I was looking down from above and I saw many churches and religions inside. All the world's churches were in that hogan. Everyone was talking in their native tongue and made a lot of noises. All the sounds were coming to me.

I then heard something being dragged. I turned and saw a pair of feet walking by and behind them was a stick being dragging along the earth. It was outside the hogan and I immediately thought that they were the feet of Jesus carrying the cross. Then the person spoke up and said, "Believe in me. That's the only way to get your body back." I thought about my body and prayed for my spirit. I knew I had seen Jesus. I saw His body but didn't see His face.

The next day I took my kids to church. I went to the preacher and told him my dream. He didn't say anything about it. I left the church and went to a medicine man and he said, "You are a true healer. That's why you had that dream. He's helping you." The medicine man told me to use the name of Jesus whenever I pray. That's what I've been doing ever since.

The Navajo way usually refers to the Great Creator, but I know this is also Jesus. That dream focused my whole life in a different way. Sometimes I get a Bible and read it out of curiosity. I read it and then I go and perform my traditional ways. I stand between these worlds and feel the wonder of it all.

My dreams taught me that the fireplace is the same as the Bible. The fireplace is also where we communicate with our ancestors and find our teachings. The peyote is a translator. It is used the same way you use a telephone to make a call. It gives you messages and helps you understand things. The peyote can tell you what your patient is talking about and what he or she is saying through the fireplace.

Prayer

When I first learned how to pray for someone, I went to our highest mountain with my whistle. The whistle was given to me by a medicine man. I looked around and saw everything down below and all the way around. I asked the Creator to teach me how to pray and to understand what I'm saying when I'm praying. I wanted to learn to deeply concentrate while praying. While I was talking in my prayers, a wind came up and blew on my face. I guess that's the experience you're supposed to have. After the wind went away, I continued praying for a long time asking for understanding. I kept repeating that request. Suddenly, I heard something and when I turned, a big elk was facing me. The elk came closer and I thought it was going to attack me, but he just came closer and closer. I kept praying with my eyes closed, and the wind came up on me again. I opened my eyes and the elk was gone. Immediately, I knew that my prayers went in all directions. The elk symbolized many lines of prayer that can be made. My husband, who watched from a distance, said that an eagle circled as I was praying. I didn't see the eagle because my eyes were closed in prayer. This is how I learned to pray and it gave me a sacred confirmation that I could fulfill the duties of a medicine woman.

A prayer goes from the east to south, west, and to the north. Then we do the center and upper ways. When you pray for a person, start on the right side first and then down to the left, followed by both feet and finally upwards. The songs work from the head on down. With a song, you're washing a patient and cleansing their body, but with a prayer, you're building them up.

When you are performing a ceremony, you can give herbs to your patient to help them feel the truth about themselves. While the patient is taking the herbs, you also have to take it because you will sing and chant the sickness out of the patient. You and the patient must take the medicine at the same time so that you can both feel certain things together. In the end, everything walks in beauty again. That's how it works.

Mother Earth and the Four Directions

When a medicine person is teaching you, you have to really listen. They have several things that they go by. For instance, it is important to learn your colors. The white is from the east, the blue from the south, the yellow from the west, and the black from the north. The four sacred mountains must also be known: Sisnaajini (Blanca Peak), Tsoodzil (Mount Taylor), Dook'ooslid (San Francisco Peak), and Dibénitsaa (Hesperus). There are two other sacred mountains which are somewhat secret and seldom mentioned. *All Creation (Rainbow) Mountain* provides a sacred door for spiritual work, and *Medicine Mountain* is where one finds many healing herbs.

Even the Mother Earth has colors. A stone's color represents its personality and they, too, belong to the four directions: white-shell (east), turquoise (south), abalone (west), and black jet (north). If a person wants to be positive, you use a stone from the east which brings a power that can help. A woman's liberation is from the north side. A new marriage or new beginning comes from the south side. This knowledge helps direct how you perform on a patient.

When you see red rock, you understand that red symbolizes our inner feelings. That's where the Mother Earth feels close to the Creator. If you come to a yellow place, yellow earth means you should show respect in that area. If you come to a green place, a place with many plants, this is where the healer is. If you're in the desert, you will find directions to create yourself with beauty. If you see white sand, that's for being more positive about things. Blue is for when you're going to have a child or when you want to grow a plant or when you want to adopt something. People sometimes need to change their mind and their attitude. There is a door in the west for change. Finally, most people don't fool around with the north because that's where evil is taken away. However, I like working with the north. It's a powerful place for change and healing.

In our tradition, we learn to work with the four directions. We are taught to enter a hogan and move in a clockwise direction. You must walk in the correct way or you'll disrespect the traditions of

White represents new beginnings and spiritual purity; blue symbolizes the life force that makes things grow; yellow suggests wisdom, spiritual blessing, and healing; black suggests the underworld, as well as rain and fertility.

These mountains are identified as: Sierra Blanca Peak in Colorado or Pelado Peak in the Sangre de Cristo Mountains near Alamosa, New Mexico, for the east; Mount Taylor in the San Mateo Range near Grant, New Mexico, for the south; Humphrey's Peak in the San Francisco Mountains near Flagstaff, Arizona, for the west; and it is uncertain, but probably Hesperus Peak in Colorado in the north.

someone's home. If you walk in the right way, you'll be greeted and treated with respect and kindness. If you don't know your four directions, you're out of whack. You're out of place. That's what my grandpa used to say. Because of my grandpa, I really know my four directions. He used to say, "Stand straight on Mother Earth and look at the four directions. What do you see?" I used to look in all four directions early in the morning because he got us out of bed and told us to go outside to say our prayers. Sometimes he told us to put water in our mouths but not to swallow it. With water in our mouths we had to run as far as we could. I think we ran for a mile and a half. Running a long time makes you want to swallow. I wanted to swallow the water. When we got back, he made us spit out the water in a glass to see how much we had left. He drew a line for the water he gave us. We hoped we would have more water from saliva. When I swallowed the water, he would say that I wasn't really focused yet and talk about the four directions. He said I should always know which way I'm standing and know my direction. He said I needed to know this to focus myself. That's how he put it.

Other Medicine People

I once tried to learn to be a medicine woman for a woman's puberty rite, which is the four-day Kinaalda ceremony that includes a special night called *All Night Prayer*. A medicine woman agreed to teach me her songs. When she came to our house and sang, it sounded kind of funny to me. I laughed about it, but according to our tradition, you are not supposed to laugh at these songs. If you laugh at a song, it will never work for you. That's what happened to me. I didn't learn the two-day Purity Chant because I laughed. I know other prayers and songs but I don't know the Purityway. During the puberty rite, I understand what they're singing about and I can sing along with them, but I can't start the song myself.

I am a strong singer in the Native American church. There I just go for it and start singing. I've had difficulty picking up some traditional songs because I laughed about them. These songs are about the frog, the snake, and the coyote. I've learned songs and prayers from many medicine people. Some of them would tell me something and say it only once. Others would say it twice. If a medicine person is talking to you and you move your head just once and look in a different direction, they might say, "You're not listening. Why should I teach you?" When I'm with another medicine person, I just sit, look, and listen to them. When they ask if I have any questions, I always say no. If you question them, they'll be after you. That's why I don't question them. I try to catch it real fast. I would then ask my husband because he and his father were medicine men. They'd further explain it to me.

My husband's father was called the Man with a Mark on His Forehead. He could heal a person with a fast heartbeat and someone with soreness all over their body. He knew the Windway, the Snakeway, the Frogway, and the Fishway.

From my childhood I remember an old blind man. Even though he was blind, he performed his medicine. He knew what kind of medicine bag it was by feeling it. He always knew where his medicine things were. When he performed on a person, he drew a wind design on the patient's body. Once I decided that he wasn't blind because he performed on people and made good drawings. So I decided to play a joke on him. We went to his place and I guess he had heard us coming. I wanted to run over to him and pull down his handkerchief. He had this nice necklace that every kid wanted. In our culture we say that when a medicine person drops their necklace, it belongs to the person who picks it up. We wanted that necklace to drop so we could pick it up. Since I knew it was connected to his handkerchief, I went for it. Before I could touch it, he got his cane and hooked my leg with it. He was fast. The cane grabbed me and pulled me towards him. He was looking at me and I shouted, "You can see, you can see!"

That joke turned back on us. You're not supposed to play around with a medicine person and try to get his stuff. He never dropped his necklace. Instead, he knew what we wanted so he untied his necklace and took a stone from it and gave it to me. That stone was very pretty. It was greenish in color. "This is what you want," he said. I nodded yes. He told me that I wasn't supposed to be doing this because if I kept on

The gift of a bead from a medicine person is special to the Diné because it is usually given to a patient as a sacred token following a ceremonial. Its possession brings protection and favor from the deities associated with the given ceremonial.

doing it, something was going to happen to me. But he gave me that stone as a gift. Ever since then, I never disrespected a medicine man.

There was another medicine man who worked with the Ghostway. He was one of the most powerful healers I ever met. He never talked, he only sang. He didn't communicate with others, but he was a powerful healer. When a person went to him he always helped them. He was a sheepherder and lived completely in nature. During his lifetime he never went to a hospital. When he died they burned his body in his house, as he wished. "Don't put me in the ground. Don't replant me. Just burn the whole thing down with me." That's what happened when he died. He dealt with a lot of bad things. He helped people visited by ghost spirits and visions of their ancestors. He was a *ghostbuster*. He went to many haunted places and communicated with the spirits of the dead.

He had a wife who was a hand trembler, but she never helped him. Years ago, there was a big gathering with many people, and he was invited to the dinner. He arrived in a horse-drawn wagon. When he got off the wagon, I saw that his hand was all black. The kids said that that's why they call him the Ghost Man, because he's always black all over. I went up to him and saw that the top of his hand was all black like smoke but clean underneath. I closely watched him. He sat away from the other people. At one point a girl cried out. I think she fell into a seizure. He immediately got up and put his hand on her with his pouch and did something right there. Everybody got scared and backed up. They were very afraid of him, but he saved the girl. I asked one of the ladies what he was doing and she said he was taking the bad spirit out of the young lady. She said it happened because the ghost chaser was there. Whenever he attended a traditional gathering, something always happened and he had to fix it. That's why he seldom went to any community events. We looked and saw that he was all black. His skin wasn't brown, it was all black, and he was even dressed in black. He was strong because he dealt with spirits most of the time. I understand that nowadays when you're spiritually sick, you blacken yourself. In the Diné tradition, we turn our body black with burned herbs to chase away the spirit. This was done to me when my husband died.

I went to a medicine man and he blackened my whole body.

That blackened medicine man only dealt with spirits. If a person wanted to talk with someone dead, he dealt with it. He had a special buckskin into which he put a bad spirit. Afterwards, he took it far away and released it. That's how he did it. I'll never forget the time when he revived the girl at the big gathering. Her tongue was all twisted and she couldn't breathe. He just put his hand around her throat as if he was choking her. He pulled something out of her, put it into his pouch, and went away. She got up and said she was dizzy and drank the water someone gave her. He was one of the truly great elders.

My husband was a quiet medicine man. He only talked if you asked him a question. He once told me to never criticize other medicine people because I don't know how they got their knowledge or what they had to go through. He greatly respected other medicine men. He never said, "That's no good, try this one." I tried not to question anyone when they were doing something because it was simply their way.

I remember a gathering that took place in Window Rock. We went there and many people were selling different kinds of herbs. My husband looked at all the plants for sale and described what each was good for. He noted the ones that were the wrong medicines. That's when he taught me to never trust anyone selling herbs in a public place. For example, there was a lady selling a medicine for the heart but it was actually a lady medicine for the mind. Also, a medicine was claimed to be for the kidneys but it was actually for the manly way. Another medicine that the seller said was for sinus headaches was actually a medicine for growing hair. David said whoever took that medicine was going to be furry.

Challenges of Life

David taught me about herbs and I followed him around and was with him when he conducted his medicine ways. I would sit by him, pray with him, and sing with him. We were a team when we did our medicine. Sometimes I miss those times. I miss him very much when I'm doing traditional medicine. I keep my sorrow inside until I'm alone. Then I cry a lot.

That's when I get mad at the world and start hitting the air. It helps relieve my pain. I go on again from there.

When we were together, he always asked me what medicine to use or what song to sing. He taught me by acting like I was the one teaching him. He said that the woman is the one with the medicine. In the Native American traditional, women are number one and that's the way my husband looked at medicine.

Many times I wake up and just think about him. I ask the same question, "Why did you go? Why? You should have told me you were going to do this." But I still don't get an answer. Not even the Holy People answer my question. The Creator is the one who took him. We were one in a spiritual way.

When we were born, we came into this world with a body. We aren't supposed to be afraid of death because we're going back to the Holy Spirit. That's what I say. That's the way David used to look at it, too. I have worked in hospitals and with older people in nursing homes. They're scared. They don't understand death. Most people don't know the life of spirit they're going into. I tell them that they're going into the circle of life.

I also learned that when you talk dirty to older people, it helps them get well. It works by making them laugh. What I tell them is that as long as you're laughing, you're living. I spend time with them, talk to them, hold their hands, and give them hugs. Some people won't come to see their old parents. I tell the old folks, "I'll be your daughter. I'll be your granddaughter. Whatever you want me to be." There's an old man named Archie who's about 90. He was sitting in a nursing home and I said, "Hello, Archie. What are you lonesome for?" He said, "My wife." I said, "Your wife? I'll be your wife." "Well, go get me some water," he said. I started laughing and I went and got some water. "Here you are, honey," I said. He started drinking the water and he felt better. When I went to get the water, I prayed that it would make him happy. I pretended to be his wife and I prayed for the water with my heart.

Old people are like children. They need more love than they ever did before. They need someone to comfort them. Sometimes I simply hold their hand and pray for them in my own way. That helps them feel better again. They call me Walking Thunder, the Navajo Indian Lady. I write letters for them and when I read the letters back to them, they say, "I didn't say that." I'd add things like, "I still care for you" and "I'm over here at the nursing home. Come and visit me." I help them say what needs to be said. Sometimes that's the job of a medicine person.

I try to teach my children to be traditional. One of them used to wear a lot of makeup, and one day while she was at school, my husband and I made a plan. I decided to get all dolled up using her makeup to paint my face. When she came home, I was cooking while wearing lipstick and all that stuff. That's what I did. My husband was laughing while he did his sandpainting. My daughter just stared at me. I walked around acting like I was very young. Finally, she said, "Mom! Take that makeup off before somebody sees you." I said, "I'm going to start wearing makeup since you're not going to quit." She immediately stopped wearing makeup. I said, "Why did you hide your beauty? That's your natural beauty under there." To this day, she doesn't wear makeup.

Another daughter came home late one evening with marks on her neck. I said, "What's that mark on your neck? Is that what they do today?" I turned to my husband and said, "Can you give me one of those too?" My husband said, "Look at how somebody ate our daughter around the neck." She didn't like the remarks. Finally, my husband asked, "Who's our new son-in-law? Bring him over. I'd like to see what kind of man he is. Or is it a girl who did that to you?" She stopped dating for a while. Whenever we went to her school we'd ask her, "Who's the guy who ate you up?" She would turn red and wouldn't talk about it. She never told us who the person was. Humor is one of the most powerful medicines for teaching and healing others.

I was particularly impressed with a cowboy movie John Wayne made about young kids. He taught them to take the cattle a long way. I have seen all his movies and I wish I could have shaken his hand. I did, however, manage to see him from a distance. He was tall. "That's my hero," I said. I taught my kids by watching his movies and paying attention to what he said to other people. I also learned how to train horses from his movies and use some of the methods he used. There are a lot of things I learned from John Wayne and I liked the way he taught.

The sacred tobacco

Taking the Evil Out

Years ago I was asked to help some people in Arizona. I went up there with my mom, my aunt, my husband, and some other relatives. I thought I was performing a little thing for them, but when I arrived, I saw all these medicine men sitting in there waiting for me. They had set the fire and were ready to go through the night. I told my husband, "I didn't come for this. I came for a little ceremony." My husband replied, "If you consider yourself a medicine woman, you'd better sit down and take time for your patients." I sat down and started the work. The hardest part was the mother and father. They were mad at each other and didn't want to talk. I told them, "I'm sorry I have to say this. You two are older than me and you've experienced more things than me. But you are expecting me to help your son, and I can't do it unless you act your age." I added, "If you two keep acting this way, we're going to have to let go of your son." Finally they got the point and cooperated with me in the medicine ways.

I found out that their son was being witched by a bad person and that that person was his own uncle. The uncle, wearing a silver headband, was sitting with us. I couldn't say, "Your uncle is the one who is killing you." I explained that someone had bewitched the boy with a crystal and by putting his picture on water. I announced that I would take my whistle and pray in the way I was taught. Then I said, "I'm going to give you two hours to straighten everything out." The uncle raised his hand and said, "I've got to go home and get some sleep. I have to herd the sheep in the morning."

I knew why he was leaving. He had to take the evil thing out. He knew who I was talking about and he was afraid. We let him leave. Two hours later when I figured he was finished, I went out and performed my prayer. The next thing I knew, that boy didn't need his oxygen. His uncle had released him from the spell. I didn't do it. I just threatened him to get it done. He knew that when a person blows on the whistle of an eagle bone that spiritual power comes forth.

When I first used my whistle, I was very surprised. I visioned a person without a body, someone made of smoke. When you take a whistle all you have to do is stand there and close your eyes and envision all the things surrounding you. That's the way the whistle works. If you don't fully believe and just do it for fun, it's not going to happen.

Medicine Traditions and Crystal Visions

My tradition has its own way of understanding health and illness. For example, consider a young person who is frightened by lightning. In the traditional way, if you ever get struck by lightning it is supposed to reawaken you. When you come to yourself, you're supposed to stay away from home. If the person instead goes straight home while he still smells of lightning, the people surrounding him can get cancer. The smell of the lightning smoke can give you cancer. It can also give you bone spurs and arthritis.

In another example, if a woman is pregnant and the moon eclipses while she's eating, her baby will have heart problems or breathing problems. If a pregnant woman sees a dead dog and kicks it or walks over it, that baby will have stomach and digestive problems. We try to avoid these kinds of situations. If a patient can't remember what happened to them, the medicine person says prayers until that patient remembers. When that person remembers, they determine how many moon changes and cycles have taken place, and they have to look back and think back for them. This helps us know what we must do to bring things back to balance.

We can find out what is wrong with a person by using a crystal.

All Diné healing ceremonies have the same goal of restoring *hozho,* a word with no direct English-language equivalent. It is a mix of the concepts of sacred, holy, blessed, balanced, and harmonious. Washington Matthews originally translated it to mean "beauty."

(Hosteen Beaal's) mediumistic ability was much in demand for locating lost articles and lost horses and sheep and in tracing kidnapped children. He had demonstrated his ability so many times and with such amazing results that no one, Indian or white, questions his unusual powers. We had occasion to seek his help three times: once when our store was robbed of more than $3,000 worth of turquoise and silver jewelry that we were holding as pawn; once to locate a crazy Navaho who had tried to kill Mrs. Nelson, a neighboring trader's wife; and again when someone had opened the gate bars of our corral and made off with our three saddle horses..... Hosteen Beaal solved all three problems. For the first he took Arthur to a cave where the jewelry and most of the money was hidden; in the second case he traced the criminal to a mountain hideout; and for the third he told us where we would find the horses. After this there was not much theft in our valley.

Franc J. Newcomb, *Hosteen Klah: Medicine Man and Sand Painter,* 1964, p. 143

It's like a TV. It helps us receive messages. Have you ever seen a big mountain when there's a fog around it? As you look at it, the images shift. It's similar to how the crystal works. You make your focus at one place, you ask questions, and you stare at it, thinking about the fog, the season, and other relevant things. That's how I receive. It's my x-ray machine. If a person says that he's very sick and doesn't know what's going on with him, I use my crystal and look at that person. I focus the person's body in that crystal. Sometimes I might see asthma. At other times it might be stomach cramps or high blood pressure. Then I ask questions in the pollen way. Is it from lightning? Or is it from the moon or sun? The one creation? The whirling rainbow? I'll focus on where he's hurting. There will be a little white lightning. That's the electricity in there that tells you what's going on. That's what you call vision into crystal.

I had a heart problem and the medical doctor told me that I wasn't going to live longer than a year. They made me wear some kind of medical device but I got tired of carrying it around. I went to He Who Walks Away, one of my teachers, to see what was really wrong with me. I found out that I was making myself sick from stress. It was weakening my body. He gave me a crystal for visioning and said that I was going to be doing it for the rest of my life. He also gave me four different kinds of corn that he cooked in the fireplace. He gave me four differently colored arrowheads so I'd be strong in four directions. He blessed me with a two-day ceremony and taught me how to use the crystal vision. He said I could use it to find a missing person.

Months later, some people asked me to find a lost girl. The people who asked were filled with doubt about the crystal and helping them almost killed me. They didn't gift me, but they asked me to do it. I don't want to go through that again so now I am more careful.

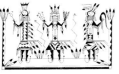

Symbol for He
Who Walks Away

Holy Wind and Lightning

He Who Walks Away taught me that there is a wind inside each person. The wind can talk to you. For example, it might make you feel that there is a highway patrol over the hill. Without thinking, you automatically slow down. That's your wind talking to you. The wind can put you in both bad and good ways. It's up to you how you work with it.

Some healing has to do with using the wind. The wind is always there. The lightning and thunder are always there. The four sacred plants, corn, tobacco, wheat, and squash are always there.

Once they performed a bear thing on me. They dressed me up, put me under a tree, and gave me plants that made me feel like I was a bear. When they finished the arrangements, the medicine man sang the Wind Song. I felt the wind go through me; the chill of the wind passed through my body.

We believe that tiny lightning can enter your body and cause you to move. If you get sick, you have to push more lightning back in there to recharge yourself. When medicine people feel the lightning, they'll get a chill or a body twitch. This is how lightning works in our healing. When lightning moves in your body, that's the Thunderway with the Wind. This is behind the twitching of a holy person.

There are Thunderways of the Wind, Cloudways of the Wind, the Four Sacred Mounds of the Wind, and the Courage Sunburst of the Wind. The Thunderways of the Wind puts a new wind back in you. It uses green herbs. The Thunder Person will be all black representing the wind from the north side.

If you pray deeply, you might hear a sacred wind. When you pray deeply, you will see what others don't see, you will hear what others don't hear. You can even see a holy person come into the room. When a person goes with the holy ways, his speaking tongue changes. The same thing happens to Christians when they speak in tongues. It is similar to our traditional ways. We might start talking in our language, but it will change to a spirit-filled way of talking. It, too, is a special wind.

When I do a performance on someone, they may feel the wind enter their body. For me, when I was being doctored, it felt like something peeling off. I couldn't move as the medicine man performed. I had a heavy feeling and couldn't move. He then said a prayer, sang a song, and blew the whistle again. I felt like he was putting me back together. Then, I was able to move.

NOTE: The Diné depict the energy of the holy wind as a holy person with horns adorned with a whirlwind headdress.

Sandpainting

We will not give
you this picture.
Men are not
as good as we;
They might
quarrel over the
picture and tear it
And that would
bring misfortune.
The black cloud would
not come again,
And the rain would not fall.
The corn would not grow.
But you may paint
it on the ground,
With the colors of the earth.

from the Navajo Creation Story

SANDPAINTING:
Diné term *'iikááh*, means
the place where the
Holy Ones "enter and go."
Sandpaintings are regarded
as sacred living entities.

Sandpaintings are also used in our healing ceremonies. I first saw a sandpainting when I was a little girl. I had just walked into a hogan and found two people sitting on the floor. They were making a painting on the ground. I asked them what they were doing and they said they were performing the medicine way. I asked, "What kind of medicine way?" One of the medicine men said, "Just look at it and you'll understand." I sat down and started eating a roasted corn. Every time I made a noise, the sandpainter would tell me to be quiet. They first made four snake designs that went up and down. The Snakeway was being used for a woman having menstrual problems. The patient could hardly stand up. She had to have people help her get up and she'd moan when she tried to move. The snakes on the painting were in the four sacred colors. They were all crooked but they were v-shaped on their body symbol. I noticed that the lips of the snakes did not connect.

I kept watching until the medicine men said they were done. The patient was told to go outside. After she left, they added more designs on the sandpainting. A smaller snake was placed in a corner. It was a King Snake. When they were finished with the extra details, they told the lady to come in. They proceeded to doctor her in the traditional way. The woman didn't want anyone to see the performance so we had to leave. I asked my grandma why they asked us to leave when they let us see the sandpainting. She said that when a medicine man is doing a healing ceremony with a sandpainting, it's up to the patient to decide whether they want other people to be present. The woman wanted privacy because they were dealing with her body

After the performance, people had a feast. I kept wondering what had happened. I was curious as I walked around the hogan. I found a little hole, but I couldn't see anything through it. They had put cloth against the hole. It was a very private occasion. When they were done, she stopped moaning and she moved with ease.

Later, as a child I saw a sandpainting in the healing way of lightning. It was a Thunder Person. I was able to watch that performance done for a newly wed couple. The man sat on the right and the woman on the left. The medicine man told them that the man is the head of the household and the woman is the one who takes care of the home. The

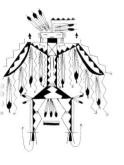

Symbol for Lightning

medicine man said, "This is not going to affect you in the future or in the past. This is just help for getting something done. If you want to do it, go for it. Now is your chance." The young couple got up and I got up too. The medicine man then allowed me to make my first rainbow there. He let me make a rainbow design on the sandpainting at the foot of the thunder, which was turquoise and red. Its border was yellow on one side and white on the other side. In the middle was a large Rainbow Person with a rainbow on his side.

The medicine man said that the rainbow symbolized their hope and ambition. The young woman wanted many kids, so the rainbow surrounding the thunder had many kids. The husband wanted his kids to respect him so it was colored yellow. He also wanted his kids to think positively. The color white was for that. The center of the painting depicted their aim to grow old together with no one but themselves. It was like putting the marriage together in a special way. The medicine man said that if they strayed from the marriage, something bad would happen.

After I made the rainbow, the medicine man said the people who helped him with the sandpainting would have more forwardness. He said that nothing would stop us from reaching our purpose. He then brought out his pollen bag. He went on to interpret the symbols and colors of the sandpainting. He made an X on each side of the thunder with his pollen. He told the husband to put his knees on a certain spot on the painting and the wife to place her knees on another spot. They had to do the same for their hands. They had to swing their bodies onto the sandpainting and sit down on it. That was the first time I ever saw such a performance. I was about ten when I witnessed it. It was a good ceremony. The couple is still alive and together.

My grandpa and uncle taught me that the sandpainting heals and that it came from the first world up to the fifth world. The first world was below the earth and when they came into the fifth world the Holy Ones recognized the four directions by finding a white cloud in the east, a blue cloud from the south, a yellow cloud from the west, and darkness to the north. Those were their colors when they first came from the world below. The first world was a holy time when people spoke and

Diné origin teachings explain how their first people journeyed through different world-realities. Presently they exist in the fifth world. These spiritual histories help orient them to a harmonious life in spite of the difficulties and challenges that come along the way.

things happened. When they got mad, they changed the cycle of the world. They learned that the world changes when disagreement and violence take place. The second world was also holy and filled with magic. The third and fourth worlds were also holy. When they came into the fifth world, however, people began to act up. So the sacred powers were taken away from them.

The first sandpaintings were done on buckskins. When the Holy Ones decided to travel from the first world, they painted messages on buckskins. Eventually these were brought into the fifth world. Then they began to draw on the rocks. After that, the Holy Ones began talking about healing and placed sacred power into sandpaintings. The first sickness they faced came from the evil ways. It was on White Shell Woman. She became very sick in this world. So they performed a dance for her. A Holy One visioned how she should be healed. He dreamed a four-day ceremony in which she throws up each morning, takes herbs, receives prayers, and so forth. This was the beginning of a chant way. They tied a feather on her head. The feather symbolized a traveler, indicating new beginnings for her life. As we say, it's challenging a life. In other words, a person must step out from sickness by pushing it away.

Grandpa told me that people were told to look at water during a performance. They called water, Earth Mirror. When they look at themselves in the Earth Mirror, they realize who they are. By looking in that glass of the earth their true self is realized. The elders say that it's usually your mind that gets confused and unclear about things. That's when we need to look in a special way to see things clearly.

One of our traditional stories tells about a man who couldn't hear anymore. He awoke one morning and was supposed to get a message from a bluebird telling him what kind of day he was going to have. The bluebird came but he didn't hear the message. He panicked and went to find help. A vision was brought for him that gave birth to another chant way—Yeibichai. As it was performed, he heard a song in the beat of the drum.

As he heard the distant drum, he started dancing. During that time in our sacred history, the people were not as we are today. They were taller and lived a more holy way of life. Some of their healing ways are

Symbol for White Shell Woman, Yolkaí Están, who was a mythological deity and the younger sister of Changing Woman, or Estsánatlehi, the most revered Diné deity.

In the Nightway Ceremonial, also called Yeibichai, references are made to special holy people called the Yei. The sandpaintings in this ceremony use images to invoke the presence of these Holy People. Similarly, the Yeibichai dancers attempt to summon the powers of the Holy People through aligning themselves with mythological narratives enacted in the songs and dances.

129

Rain Boy in the land-beyond-
the-sky was instructed for the Hail Chant;
'You will not make paintings in this form in the
future. Instead you will use powdered rock—dark,
blue, yellow, white, pink, brown, and red. If we give
you the paintings on the stuff we use, they will wear out.
So it is better to make them of sand each time anew.

Gladys A. Reichard, The Story of the Navajo Hail Chant, 1944, p. 147

Preparation

From top to bottom:
grinding stone; sifting
sand; choosing colors;
leveling the surface;
making a mark to
hold my focus.

A sandpainting created to help a woman become independent and strong.

133

THE RITUALISTIC PROCESS

may be likened to a spiritual osmosis

in which the evil in man and the good of

deity penetrate the ceremonial membrane

[sandpainting] in both directions, the former

being neutralized by the latter, but only if the

exact conditions for the interpenetration are fulfilled.

One condition is cleanliness, the ejection of evil so that

the place it occupied may be attractive to good powers.

The changer's ultimate goal is to identify the patient

with the supernaturals being invoked. He must become

one with them by absorption, imitation, transformation,

substitution, recapitulation, repetition, commemoration, and

concentration. The purpose of sandpaintings is to allow the

patient to absorb the powers depicted, first by sitting on them,

next by application of parts of the deity to corresponding parts of

the patient—foot to foot, knees to knees, hands to hands, head to

head. In some chants parts of the drypainting may be slept on to give

more time for absorption; sleep seems to aid the process. The chanter

applies the bundle items [sacred medicine objects] to the body parts of

the gods, then touches parts of the patient's body with his own—foot to

foot, hand to hand, shoulder to shoulder in the ceremonial order—and

finally with the bundle equipment; this is an elaborate rite of identification.

The powers, represented by the sandpainting, are conveyed indirectly by

the chanter through the bundle equipment and his own body to the patient's,

all because the chanter has obtained power to do this by his knowledge.

Gladys A. Reichard, "Navajo Religion: A Study of Symbolism," *Bollingen Series*, no. 18, 1963, pp. 112–113

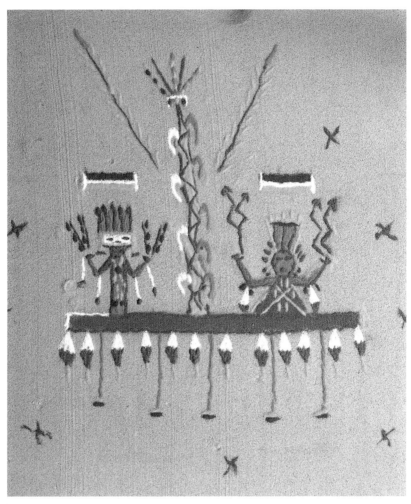

**SANDPAINTING USED
FOR HELPING A PERSON
UNDERSTAND THEIR LIFE**
The female is depicted on the right
and the male on the left. The twelve
feathers symbolize the twelve sacred
stages of a person's developmental life.

still practiced through the symbols of the sandpainting. To this day, if a person has lost their hearing, we use the Yeibichai Dance.

Another traditional sandpainting is associated with the Fire Dance. It is a large, beautiful sandpainting. I don't think anyone has ever photographed it because I have never seen a picture of it. This sandpainting can treat many patients, by them sitting on the sandpainting. When you look at it from a distance, it's the most beautiful thing you could ever see. It has corn, fancy dancers, a ribbon dancer, and other things. All the sandpaintings you could make with healing symbols are on it.

My husband and I witnessed a performance with this sandpainting. Many patients were sitting on it and each had a cloth over their head. There was also a dancer and you would think he would mess up the sand while he was dancing, but he didn't. There were drawings of feet for him to step on while dancing. He appeared light as a feather and looked very holy. He looked as if he couldn't harm or interrupt anything. The medicine man conducting the performance told us not to be happy about what we observed. He said we should look at the painting with no feeling. Any feeling might reverse itself because the dancer was a holy person within the reality of the song and prayer.

We were just looking at the sandpainting, but it was so beautiful that I couldn't help having a strong feeling about it. I opened my mouth in awe and started feeling something. The medicine man came over and said, "As soon as you feel something, let me know and I'll give you a medicine." I couldn't help but feel overwhelmed with wonder. The dancer looked as if he was flying. He went to the patients and gave each one medicine. I, too, had to be given a medicine.

Our people say that the way to show your gratitude and respect to a medicine person is by feeding them and treating them like they are at home. We never say thank you to a medicine person for the help they give us. A lady once said to a medicine man, "I know I'm not supposed to say this, but I want to say thank you." The medicine man just took his things and left. He cut off the ceremony and said, "You disrespected my medicine. In the beginning, I told you not to say that. I already knew you were grateful because you fed me and made me feel at home. Now you say 'thank you' to me and that's no good." And he just walked out.

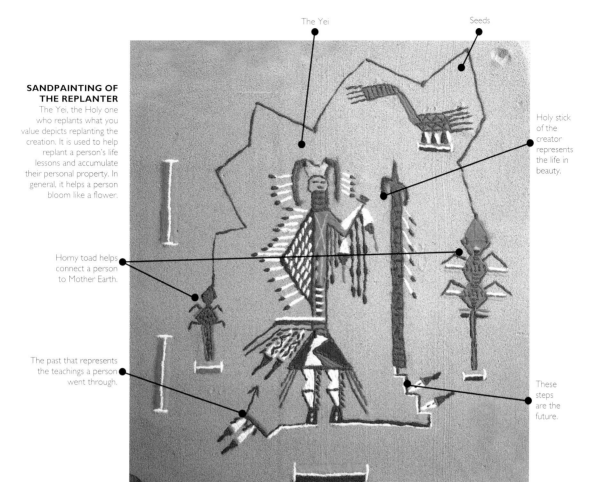

The Yei

Seeds

SANDPAINTING OF THE REPLANTER
The Yei, the Holy one who replants what you value depicts replanting the creation. It is used to help replant a person's life lessons and accumulate their personal property. In general, it helps a person bloom like a flower.

Holy stick of the creator represents the life in beauty.

Horny toad helps connect a person to Mother Earth.

The past that represents the teachings a person went through.

These steps are the future.

A medicine person can receive a smoke from the sacred tobacco as thanks. It's also appropriate for them to receive gifts, including cash. That's how traditional people work.

I learned that there are about 745 sandpaintings used for healing ceremonies. The creation story has another 600 sandpaintings used to teach children about our traditional ways. We talk about Mother Earth and Father Sky and explain the changing world and the meaning of lightning. There are many rules and prohibitions concerning healing sandpaintings, whereas the creation story has more freedom. You can do whatever you want with it, but you still have to be blessed to do the creation story sandpaintings.

The first sandpainting I ever made was the Pollen Boy. My father-in-law, who is medicine man, watched me as I made it. His staring made me very nervous and a drop of my sweat dropped on the sandpainting. He said I had to erase the whole thing because my sweat dropped on it. That was it, it was over. I erased the whole thing and then he said a prayer and sang a song over me. I was supposed to wait four days before trying it again. I wanted to try again that same day so I gave him a turquoise earring. It was the only thing I had. He looked at me and said, "You better do it." I sat back down that day and started it all over. I took a scarf from his pocket and put it around my head so my sweat wouldn't drop on the painting.

I started with my rainbow this time. He was really watching me and asked me to explain everything I drew. The only thing I messed up were the feathers. Two feathers were on the left instead of on the right. And there was supposed to be three antennae instead of two. You cannot make that mistake on a healing ceremony sandpainting. But on the Creation Story you can make all the mistakes and just get new sand and erase it. But in a healing ceremony, pollen is already on the floor where the sandpainting is going to made. They have already given the corn to Mother Earth and you can't take it back from Mother Earth or take back the pollen from the earth to restart. If you make a design crooked in some way, it's your fault and it's your problem because you made it.

My father-in-law, who taught me how to make sandpaintings, knew how to heal sores and cancers. One of his favorite sandpaintings was the Pollen Boy. The reason why it was his favorite was because he was a giving person. He liked to help people. That's how he saw himself. In our worldview, how a person does a sandpainting represents how they see themselves. When supervising my first sandpainting, he first gave me orders to do it his way. I messed up. When I painted my own rainbow, it worked the right way. In the beginning he had given me overly specific instructions to mix me up. I had done what he said and messed up. That was his teaching. The next time I tried, I began to do it my own way. He didn't say anything because my rainbow was there. I went on with my own design of the story. I also made a little gourd thing and tied bluebird feathers on it to make the sandpainting real.

THE POLLEN BOY is a spirit force masked and wrapped in pollen.

The gifts required for major ceremonials which consist of numerous rites and performances, often require food and animals for a feast to feed the attending community as well as money, which in the case of long chants, may be over a thousand dollars.

Thus the presentation of the origin myth in song, prayer, and sandpainting is not only for the purposes of remembrance and education, but to allow the patient to identify with those symbolic forces which once created the world, and by entering into them to re-create himself in a state of health and wholeness.

Donald Sandner
Navajo Symbols of Healing
1979, p. 111

A sandpainting of the healing ways can be really detailed or it can be plain. It's up to the medicine person, depending on how they make it. You look at the patient and see what is necessary. You then put the appropriate design inside. That's how the sandpainting gets designed. The details of each one are uniquely tailored to the particular situation. The general theme is always the same, but the details depend on the patient's situation. That's how I do mine with the Pollen Boy—by looking at the patient and then doing it. I put my own details into it based on how I think the patient can be helped.

I'm told that there are only nine medicine women who do the sandpaintings for healing. One woman knows how to sing over the sandpaintings. I know how to pray over them. Another woman uses the whistle, while another uses smoke. None of us are alike because there are different ways of doing the healing and helping the patient.

As I mentioned before, the original designs came from the first world. Other designs came later from people who visioned things. All the details of my sandpaintings come from my dreams. The way I see it and the way I understand it comes with me. Another medicine person may have the same general figure, but the design details come from my dreams.

When I'm going to perform a sandpainting on a person, I usually ask for a dream. If it doesn't come, I don't do a sandpainting. If I have to wait many days for that dream to come, I have to wait. Sometimes it can take five days. I follow what my dream tells me and I never question it. When I vision something, it happens. I don't play with it. Sometimes it scares me but I have to go by what it tells me.

The sandpaintings I like to perform are the Whirling Logs, Thunder, and Sunbursts. Those three sandpaintings are my favorite ones. I also perform Walk in Beauty. There's a little song and a prayer for Walk in Beauty. The Courage Sunburst is for people who hesitate to do things; it gives you courage to do things. The Thunder Ceremony includes drinking herbs, meditating, self-understanding, prayers, and smoke. It is for someone who wants to accomplish something. One client wanted to become a school principal. I did the performance on her and now she's the head of the school. Another patient wanted to be a councilman. He's now a councilman of the Navajo Nation. He's still my patient.

WALK IN BEAUTY SANDPAINTING

The Difference Between Commercial and Ceremonial Sandpaintings

There are differences between sandpaintings made for commercial art (or public demonstration) and those used for healing ceremonies. A sacred sandpainting contains power that can be dangerous if not respected or treated appropriately. Such a painting can never be permanent because someone could make a mistake in its presence and bring harm to themselves or others. That's why we only make them under carefully supervised procedures and never allow them to be made permanent. Sacred sandpaintings attract the Holy People and if they see that we are not being respectful of the old ways, they might bring sickness to us.

When we make a ceremonial sandpainting, we do so upon a bed of clean, riverbed sand that has been smoothed with a weaving batten. Only sacred ceremonial sandpaintings use this natural riverbed sand. Commercial sandpaintings are not mixed with riverbed sand.

When we make a commercial sandpainting, we will change the sacred designs so that they are imperfect. This takes away their sacred perfection and leaves them without power. We can do this by substituting different figures in the design. We never draw the image of a powerful deity for a commercial sandpainting. We typically use Holy People who are are easygoing and good natured such as the Rainbow People.

There are many ways to make a holy design imperfect. Some people change some of the directionality in the design or use different colors. A detail may be eliminated or extra details may be added. Commercial sandpaintings allow us to use our imagination to add new things to the designs. Some of the brighter colors used for commercial sandpaintings are not used for the ceremonial designs. These are some of the ways we alter the sacred designs and make them imperfect. The Holy Ones leave these designs alone so they are safe to sell to others.

My favorite sandpainting, *The Four Directions*, consists of four Replanters with lightning that moves everything in a clockwise direction. This is used to help put a person's life back in order, particularly when they are under great stress of personal difficulty.

THE FOUR DIRECTIONS

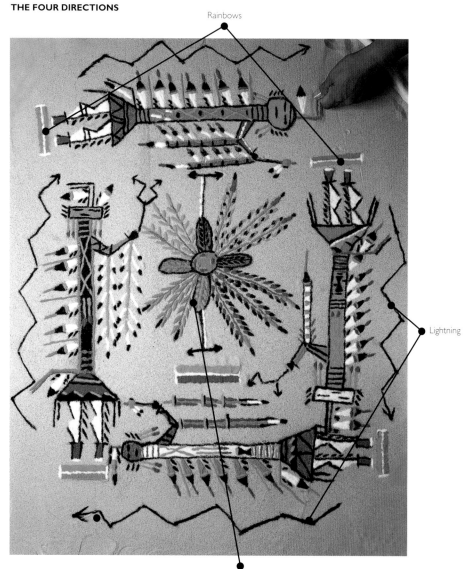

Rainbows

Lightning

Four sacred tobacco plants

Another one of my favorite sandpaintings.

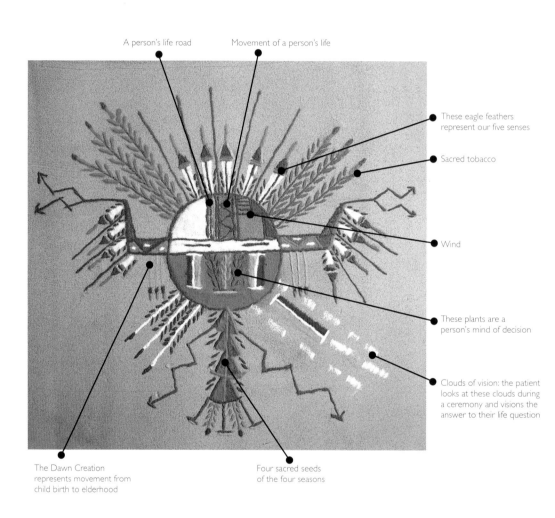

A person's life road

Movement of a person's life

These eagle feathers represent our five senses

Sacred tobacco

Wind

These plants are a person's mind of decision

Clouds of vision: the patient looks at these clouds during a ceremony and visions the answer to their life question

The Dawn Creation represents movement from child birth to elderhood

Four sacred seeds of the four seasons

The Warrior Sandpainting is used for hunting night.

The Replanter of
Two Rainbow Ways

Father Sky

Holy Boy from the
East to the West

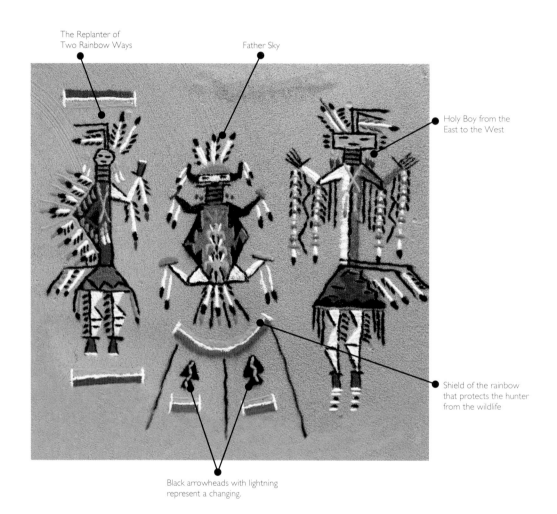

Shield of the rainbow
that protects the hunter
from the wildlife

Black arrowheads with lightning
represent a changing.

THE WARRIOR SANDPAINTING

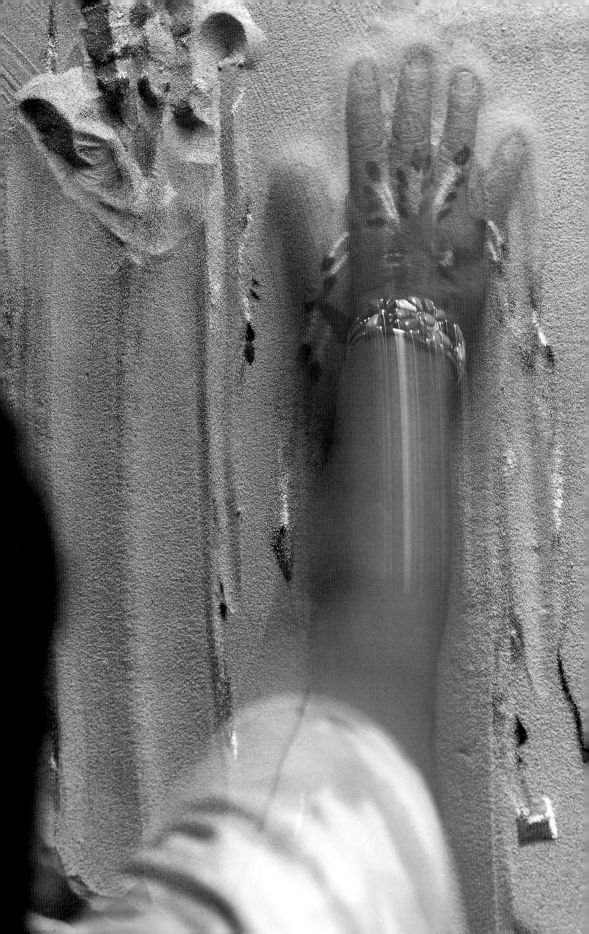

Being
a Medicine
Woman

A young girl was very ill
with tuberculosis and her
parents consulted a diviner. He
gazed steadily at a star and sang.
Suddenly, he saw the star open
with a blazing hogan in the midst
of it and around it. There was no
overcoming such an omen and
without a vestige of hope the
man decreed that the girl would
die. In less than a month his
prophecy had been fulfilled.
If it had been possible for the
girl to get well, he would have
seen a 'white sign come around
the hogan like frost.'

Gladys A. Reichard, *Social Life of
the Navajo Indian*, 1928, p. 149

When I'm in deep contact with my patient, my heart and body movement slow down, and my head feels like there's a hole in it. If it's a little hole, it's easier to focus. Once it gets bigger, I have to concentrate more to keep my focus. When a spirit appears, it can look like a regular person. Unlike a person, however, it can pass through walls and even through a human being. Sometimes they will hold your hand in a ceremony. They can also sprinkle water on people. Those are the Water Messengers. They won't hurt you, but they make you tingle and feel cold or warm when they pass through you.

Sometimes I suck out illnesses. When you take it out, it's ugly. Sometimes you have to turn away when you take it out. The first thing you do is throw it in the fire and burn it. You don't keep it. It looks like a worm from prehistoric times. It's either yellow or white in color.

Medicine people must take special care of themselves. I never ran around and never drank. However, I've done a lot of mischief and practical jokes. For instance, years ago when I was young, a group of women were all naked in the sweathouse. They were all singing away. I threw a stick in there and shouted, "Here comes a snake!" They came flying out of the sweathouse and all the guys saw their breasts. That was funny. One of the old ladies got a pitchfork and started chasing us. We took off. That's the kind of mischief I made. I was curious about what people's bodies looked like. I found out in truly funny ways. I was amazed how those old ladies crawled into the sweathouse, barely able to move as they went in, but when I said, "Snake!" and pushed that stick in there, it was as if years melted away and much younger ladies ran out of there.

I'm like a bear seeking direction. The bear looks at the stars to find his way. I always look at the stars and try to get my answers. I just look at the stars with a positive mind and think about what I want to do.

My grandpa taught me about the circle of life. It's a different understanding from the talk about heaven and hell and the end of the world. One night I dreamed about the future. The world will not end. Rather, the world is going to change. Part of the United States is going to be missing. There won't be a Maine or a California. One of my elders says there will only be four cities at that time. The world won't change with fire and it won't change with thunder. Some people will survive and some will not survive. The people who made preparations will survive. That's how I vision the future. One should get ready by paying attention to only one day at a time. Do you know how to build a fire? Do you know how to stay warm? Do you know how to camp? You need to know these things in order to survive. It's a wise idea to live in the wild right now.

Nowadays Mother Earth is angry. She is very disturbed. She doesn't want to let anything grow on her. I keep telling the medicine people to cut the four sacred stones to get ready for the planting season. We put the stones out for the wind in all directions and say a prayer and a song for them.

Once we put a Rain Girl and a Rain Boy at our house. We asked another medicine man to perform the four-day ceremony. We furnished the food and people came. Many people helped. Then, the rain came. Everyone with land put four sacred stones out where the frogs live and where the plants grow. After we did that, we started having rain again. We didn't do a Rain Dance. Our way is the quiet path of the stone ways.

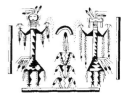

Rain Girl and Rain Boy

Some people say not to perform on white people. My husband and I always looked at all people as God's children. We were one in the beginning but grew roots in different ways. In the end we will return to being one again.

Years ago some people became jealous of my power and tried to put a curse on me. They drew a picture of me on a stick and put the stick in a coffin and buried it in a cemetery next to my sister's grave. I had a breathing problem for a while. Various things were done for me, but nothing helped. When I received my crystal, I saw what was going on. I went to the graveside and talked to my sister buried there. I asked for her blessing and asked her to kick out anyone who fooled around with her grave. My husband and I dug up the object and burned it.

The best way to overcome these things is by burning them. If you take something out of a patient, you shouldn't show it to them. If the patient wants to get well, they don't need to know what was removed. Just go and burn it.

One evening, my husband and I drove back from a Blessingway Ceremonial and another car rammed our car on purpose. We were also threatened with a gun. All we did was put our faith in the Creator and

If the patient be a man, he is stripped to the breech-cloth (a female patient retains her clothes). He has a single breath-feather, taken from the shoulder of an eagle, tied to his hair. As soon as it is tied on he begins to tremble violently (or should tremble) as if under the influence of a hypnotic spasm . . . if the patient is seized with trembling, which is usually the case, the shamans say they know the malady is caused by the gods casting a spell on the patient; but if he is not thus seized they must seek some other cause.

Washington Matthews,
The Night Chant: A Navajo Ceremony, 1902, p. 115

asked Him to shield us. We got out of the situation without being hurt even though the man tried to tip our car over. He wore a mask and clearly wanted trouble. We just kept on driving and praying. If you walk in a holy way, people will mess with you and try to hurt you. If you show that you don't give a shit about what happens, you'll get stronger and they won't bother you as much.

I once had a patient with diabetes. One day, she gave up and didn't want to live. I went over to her house with peaches and crackers. When I was going inside her house, I saw something. A ghostlike person—a giver or a taker of life—stood over the patient. He looked at me and pointed with his hand. He indicated that she was going to die in three days. I cried right there. I tried to plead with the holy person in my prayers but he turned away from me and never turned back. He showed me that she was dying from something under her skin. I ran up to her and undid her clothes. Sure enough, there was something deep under her skin. I don't know what it was.

Another experience that shook me up was when I encountered the spirits of the little Anasazi people. Years ago, my late husband David and I came back from Gallup and decided to take a walk on the hill near our home. David told me there were a lot of arrowheads there and I went to find my own. As I walked toward the old Indian ruins, I found one next to a piece of ancient pottery. As I stooped to pick it up, I saw someone's feet. They were small so I assumed it was a child. Slowly I looked up. There, standing in front of me, were several short adults with long hair. They told me to leave the arrowhead alone. I didn't pick it up but backed up as they walked toward me. I looked again at their feet and noticed they weren't touching Mother Earth. They were gliding. I closed my eyes, but I could still see them. They were dressed in white—perhaps buckskin—holding some kind of an arrow. It was a bone arrow with thread on it. I was scared and by the time they disappeared, my body started to shake. I went home crying and told my husband what I had seen. We had two interpretations of what happened. Some medicine men told us that it was a blessing for me to have seen them. Another medicine man said it was bad luck.

When I see an eagle I communicate with it. When I see a coyote I always give him a problem to work out. When I hear an owl I always release it. Those are the animals I have contact with. I don't eat the animals that I communicate with. I don't eat owl, eagle, coyote, or crow. But I eat deer. Snake is an evil to me and I leave it alone. It brings bad luck for me. When I see a snake I have to kill it. I won't let it crawl on its jolly old way. When you kill an arrow snake you get rain. That's good for planting. When my kids see an arrow snake, I ask them to chase and kill it and leave it for the eagle. When I see any snake, I kill it and leave it for the eagle. That's my way of gifting him. I place it on top of a rock.

There are special places that are sacred to me. There is a sacred mountain where I go for prayer. At the mesa there's a sacred rock. I go there and talk to it. There are other places where medicine men place their stones. You don't run to a sacred space every day. You only go at special times.

Once, my husband dropped me off at a place and told me to stay there for four hours. He then took off. When he came back and picked me up, I was completely rested and restored. It was that kind of a place. You go there and say your prayers, close your eyes, and forget about life. As you close your eyes, you focus yourself. That's what he told me to do. You must also make sure to put your herbs at that place.

The sacred things I use were given to me as gifts. My eagle whistle, flute, and feathers were all gifts. These are earned by helping people. One of my gifts was the teaching that all healers should be truthful to their patients. Secondly, they should listen to their inner feelings, bringing forth understanding. Thirdly, always remember your four directions.

A long time ago my grandpa told me that the truest medicine person would only eat the leaves of Mother Earth's creation. The truest medicine person would not eat meat. He used to say that when a medicine person eats meat, sickness more easily comes upon him. He said that there was only one medicine person who was this true. They called him Pure. He never ate meat and he was as tall as a green bean. He had straight posture and carried his bow and arrow on his back. He never rode horses to get to places. He just ran.

I still eat meat. I'm not that pure. However, I believe that the

Creator is protecting me. I still have ceremonies done for me if I make a mistake in my ceremony or if I want to challenge something. However, I never make an effort to do a ceremony just for protection. Some Navajo medicine people have objects they use for protection. They may use arrowheads, eagle feathers, sacred rings, a cross, or a special medicine. I think I'm shielded every time I have a traditional thing done for someone. Because after each ceremony you're back into beauty—a natural state of peace and harmony—and that shields you.

The day I became a medicine woman, many women were happy. Our women like to deal with medicine women rather than medicine men. They can more easily say how they feel and they're more open. Nevertheless, I believe medicine men and women are equal.

I didn't choose to be a medicine woman. I got it through my sickness. As a little girl, I imitated medicine men and women. People would say that so-and-so was sick and I'd pretend that I was a medicine woman and start singing crazy songs. I'd say rhymes like *Mary Had a Little Lamb* in a certain way over a person. Or a medicine man would say something and I'd reverse it, saying it four times. I used to work on cats and dogs or any animal that got hurt.

Symbol for a
Medicine Person

Now one of my grandchildren who is a twin does the same thing. She breaks off a plant and says, "You'll be okay, Grandma." Then she puts her hand on me and says, "Oh, Grandma, I'm taking your headache out." She says this even when I don't have a headache. I say, "Okay, I feel better." Then she goes on her merry way.

I usually use two medicines for a sickness. One is taken before the other. I have an *encouragement medicine* and a *feather medicine*. Each medicine has a certain name. There's even a *ghostbuster medicine* and an *eagle medicine*. I learned about medicines from my grandma, my grandpa, and other medicine people. I always make medicines before a big performance. There we ask one another, "What's this plant good for?" We use most of the plants that grow on our mountain. I am particularly knowledgeable about *lightning medicine*. There's also a medicine we give to sheep so they'll have twins. Asthma is a water thing. It requires a water plant, which is known as a *green medicine* because it turns green. It leaves a bitter taste in your mouth. Water

Riccardo Cha

Darryle

Barbara
with Rocehlle

Ky

Nicole

Larry Bidtah

medicine addresses the wind. That's why we use it on asthma. We use another kind of medicine for ulcers. Each medicine has its own color, which we take into consideration for treatment.

When I started to become a medicine woman, two medicine men sent me to a mountain for four days. One of them was the man who gave me the crystal vision. I had to climb the mountain without food and water and then survive for four days. It rained and the rain gave me water. I ate the top of a yucca plant and built a fire in the old way. I was very alive.

On the first night, I walked around in the middle of the mountain. I didn't see anything that first night. On the second night, I walked around again. And on the third night, I heard a mountain lion growling. I only heard it but didn't see it. On the fourth day, I went to the very top of the mountain. It rained again and I saw lightning in all the different directions. All I did was pray. I didn't care if anything happened. I didn't have any special holy experience. It was just me, the rain, and the wind. That's it. Nothing. The medicine men said I would feel something, but I didn't. It was a test and I didn't feel anything.

Later, I had to go without water for four days. But, I was allowed to drink plant juice. That was my water. On the fourth day, my head felt unusual. I felt like a zombie. When I came down, the medicine men did something on me and the feeling went away. I told them what it felt like, but they only said, "You'll find out in your own time."

When a person goes to a medicine person and says they want to learn the medicine way, we first do a crystal vision on them. We gather the medicine people to check out the person. Then a challenge, like a Vision Fast, is given. If you can see the vision, you're welcome to have it. The knowledge is God's creation, not ours. Some medicine people will say no to someone who wants to learn. But for me, I can't say no if God wanted that person to do what I do. I can't stand in God's way. When I teach someone, I show them how to use a whistle, what kind of prayers to say for certain things, and all that. The sickness you have in your body is the payment for the things you will treat as a traditional medicine person. If you have asthma, you'd probably be helping people with asthma. I help people with heart problems because that was my sickness.

According to Clyde Kluckhohn and Leland C. Wyman (in *An Introduction to Navajo Chant Practice*, 1940), some Diné herbalists know between three and four hundred plants that can be used for healing and ceremonies.

A person who wishes to learn a chant signifies his decision by strewing sand (a special kind probably) in the hogan of the teacher and steps on it. Then he rolls pollen in four balls and both teacher and student eat it. After that they may begin the practice. The time of learning depends on the length of the change, but it takes more than a year to learn a five-day chant. They work on it when they have time at night.

Gladys A. Reichard, *Social Life of the Navajo Indians*, 1978, p. 146

My Teacher Speaks

I am Don Hoskie, one of Walking Thunder's teachers. The people call me He Who Walks Away. I'm 100 years old. I gave her the crystal vision and taught her sandpaintings and the Warrior Prayers and other songs. Now I want to teach her eight more songs and some more prayers. I want to get all of this together for her before I die.

You can't choose to be a medicine person. You must be chosen. If you are chosen, the medicine people should bless you. In my prayers the only thing I ask for is healing. I never ask for money. I don't really care for it. I was taught that money is trouble. Doing things right is the only way.

I started learning traditional medicine when I was ten. I never went to school. I just followed the medicine people around and learned from them. My real teacher, however, is the Creator. I heal people by following what the Creator says. I don't believe in paper licenses for doctors. The Creator never had that. The paper is for those who don't have confidence in the Creator. When a patient comes to me, I am confident that the Creator's going to help me in healing that patient. I don't want Walking Thunder to have a piece of paper. She should only trust the Creator when she helps a patient. A lot of people have done wrong things with the medicine way because they didn't follow the Creator. You must concentrate when you sing and pray, asking the Creator for help.

I passed on my knowledge to five people. Two of them have died and only three are left. Walking Thunder is one of my successors. I gave her the traditional ways for helping patients.

After all the performances and doctoring I've done, I now feel 200 years old. Whenever I'm in a ceremony and it's strong, I feel a wind come into my body. The wind is with me all the time. Sometimes I feel like I'm going to become Jesus, that's how strong the wind can be. I know it isn't true, but that's how I feel inside.

WALKING THUNDER, REMEMBRANCES OF HE WHO WALKS AWAY: When I first met He Who Walks Away, I was very sick. I was not a healthy woman. My husband and his sister were holding me up when we walked in and asked him to help me. I told him that I'd been sick all the time and that I'd paid many medicine men, but I didn't get any better. He asked, "Do you know why?" He then told me to come and sit by him and he asked for my hand. I put my hand in the middle of his hand and he held it for about five minutes. Then he said, "Do you know what makes you sick? And do you know what people don't see? The true healer is in you and a spirit is making you sick. You are supposed to help other people, but you are rejecting it and you don't understand it." He then told me that he was going to perform a ceremony and that he wanted me to stay for several days.

I gave him the necklace I was wearing and told him that I had no money. He started singing and giving me herbs. I felt worse that first day. On the second day, I felt lighter, and by the time he was finished, I was cured and I walked out without anyone helping me.

He chewed on an herb and then spit it into my mouth. He said, "This is for you to understand the traditional way and for you to know the prayers and to understand the prayers." Each time he performed a prayer he told a story that explained what the prayer was about. Each time he made a sandpainting, he also told a story. He roasted four sacred corns: white, blue, red, and a mixed color. He cooked them in hot ashes and when they were cooked, he put it in our mouths one at a time as he sang and did his prayers.

He made my husband sit down and touched David's heart. David immediately fell over. He then started chanting, singing, and praying until David came back up. He Who Walks Away gave the trembling hand to David. You could feel the spirit throughout his ceremony. Sometimes it was cold and then it warmed and then it would get very cold again.

He knows the sandpainting prayer ways, crystal vision, the Yeibechai way, hand trembling, the Fire Danceway, the Lightningway, and all kinds of ceremonials. He also sucks things out of a person with his mouth. He always wore a red headband when he performed ceremonies.

He warned me that a lot of people would talk against me and criticize me when I took up the medicine way. He said not to mind them because I would be doctoring the people through the Creator. "If they criticize you," he said, "then they're criticizing the Creator."

He told me that all the holy people in the four directions will help me doctor others. He taught me that when you do a crystal vision, you're supposed to use your five senses. It's about smelling, tasting, hearing, seeking, and feeling. You must use all your senses when you do crystal vision.

I first tested the crystal vision on my little brother. He had been missing from home for two weeks and my mother was trying to find him. She had asked a lot of medicine people to help her, but they kept telling her that he was going to come back. My mom spent a lot of money trying to find him. Then she came to me and said, "You know how to do the crystal vision. Go find out where your little brother is."

We sat down, burned some charcoal, and then we started doing the crystal vision. I did my prayers as He Who Walks Away had taught me. I found out that he was in a ditch somewhere near a store. I said, "He's gone. He's not on this world. He's somewhere else."

My mother didn't believe me. Sure enough, someone found him in a ditch and called the Navajo police. His body was identified by a birthmark. If a person does not believe you and they think harshly of you, it can come back to you. This happened to me and I got my sickness again. I had to go back to He Who Walks Away and tell him what happened. He sang some songs and got me well again. I know who killed my brother because the crystal vision showed me. But I kept still and decided to leave things alone.

About a month or so later, my aunt's son got lost and the FBI tried to find him. My family asked me again to do a crystal vision. I agreed and in my concentration, I heard shoveling, coughing, and the sound of plastic being moved around. I saw him being buried. When I told my aunt, she had the same reaction as my mom. She said I had put a spell on my cousin. I replied, "If you don't believe me, then go tell the police to dig up the grave." They dug it up and found him with no clothes, wrapped in plastic. Someone had stabbed him with a knife.

He Who Walks Away received his name because of the way he deals with his patients. If he has a feeling that a patient does not believe him or is testing him, he'll just gather his stuff and walk out. He'll simply stop in the middle of the ceremony and walk out without any questions.

He walks away and won't help them. People say to him, "Hey, why haven't you finished yet?" He just turns around and says, "Why should I help you? You don't believe me. You just lost your money. That's it." No matter how far he has to walk, he walks. That's how they gave him the name. He is one of the great medicine men.

One day when David and I visited him, he told us we were going eagle hunting on top of a certain hill. When we got there, he told us to stand like tree stumps. We tried but couldn't do it. He said, "Be natural. Be yourself. You're a stump already." He stood there, held up his arms, and started singing. Pretty soon an eagle flew down and sat on his arm. While singing, he pulled out some feathers. He pulled out four feathers and then some little feathers to tie onto his gourd. He put pollen in the eagle's mouth while it made noises. He waved his hand and the eagle took off. We watched the eagle circle clockwise, all the way up into the sky until we couldn't see him. He Who Walks Away taught me about the Eagleways. A living eagle feather is more holy than an eagle that's been shot or trapped. The eagle is a lifeline to the Creator. When we use the eagle feather and whistle, it puts a line between the Creator and you like a thread. You can't see it because it's invisible.

Some people were jealous of He Who Walks Away and said he was a witch doctor, but he never feared them. He was very powerful. He could use a robin feather, like a lock pick, to get inside any building. He could also use that robin's feather to go inside a person's body. He said that was the hardest thing he learned.

Years ago, He Who Walks Away visioned that one day a white man would fight for us and learn our ways. He said, "I'll meet him before I die." He taught me to follow the Creator, not the rules of other people. Sometimes people say I don't always follow the rules. I believe that I must follow whatever direction the Creator gives.

In all the creation and all the life you will go through, know that the beauty is ahead of you. As you walk, the beauty is behind you, below you, and above you. That's the way you should think about yourself. Entering the beauty is realizing that you're in the beauty. You must fully appreciate the life that the Creator has given you and take care of it. That's entering the beauty.

Opposite: Symbol for *Enter into Beauty*

In Beauty before me I walk,

In Beauty behind me I walk,

In Beauty below me I walk,

In Beauty above me I walk,

In Beauty all around me I walk,

It is finished in beauty,

It is finished in beauty,

It is finished in beauty,

It is finished in beauty.

Beauty Way Chant, Diné Benediction

The mountains,

I become part of it . . .

The herbs, the evergreen,

I become part of it.

The morning mists, the clouds,

the gathering waters,

I become part of it.

The dew drops, the pollen,

I become part of it.

Afterword

Blessing Ordination Point

Gathering sand, spilling story,
Making new ground.

Trails of pollen, hogan's open door.
Circles of prayer, whirls of wind.

Moving the Origin,
Emergence, and Beauty.

Mark the perfection, cleanse
the moment,
Bring down Father Sky,
Send up Mother Earth.

In the sacred crossings,
Thunder and Lightning,
Holy ways.

Each step brings it back,
Relationships on track.

Blessing the walk,
Carrying the talk,
All day long.

Enter the Beauty
all directions,
all ways.

B.K.

About a decade ago, I had a dream that made no sense to me at the time. In the dream I saw a hazy background of sand with a vague design, but before I could focus on it, a deep voice spoke three words that awakened me, as if spoken by someone in my bedroom. These words were uttered strongly and distinctly, "Blessing Ordination Point."

The next day I went to a used-book store and found a book that included a discussion of the Blessingway Ceremonial associated with the Diné culture. It had a photograph of a sandpainting showing entry into the pollen way of life. I felt I had stumbled upon a resonant association with my dream, having to do with initiating a journey, an ordination, into another way of seeing the world.

A week later, I had a related dream. This time I vividly saw myself sitting on the middle of a sandpainting inside a hogan. The medicine man was wearing a red scarf around his forehead and waving the feathers of an eagle. He looked toward me and said, "Enter into Beauty." I again awakened upon hearing the uttered words, feeling a strong sense of renewal and vitality. This dream confirmed my previous assumption that my inner being was being drawn to the teachings of the Diné.

That year brought several invitations to the southwest. I gave a talk on global healing traditions at a hospital in Winslow, Arizona and met several Diné medicine men. I also met a young man who taught Navajo language at a high school and college in Flagstaff. We became friends and he encouraged me to follow the dreams.

Over the years, I met other medicine people in that part of the world, but I didn't experience the connection that signaled the person I was trying to find. Step by step, however, dreams continued to provide direction. I dreamed of a piece of petrified wood that my grandfather had given me when I was a boy. In the dream, the wood was sitting next to my bed, which is where I actually keep it, and it began to vibrate at a very high frequency, causing the room to be filled with a loud pitched sound. As the dream continued, this loud pitch became the means through which my grandfather could have a voice and speak to me. He told me to immediately go to the southwest and purchase a piece of land. The dream was so powerful and demanding, that my wife and I

The Medicine Way by
Leerolline Burke, 2000

followed its advice. We immediately took off to the southwest and to our great surprise, found a plot on the rim of a canyon.

Months later, when we went back to visit our spot of wilderness, I developed a strong intuition that we should not search for a Diné medicine man, but a Diné medicine woman. It was difficult enough to find a medicine man who would talk with you about spiritual concerns due to the secretive nature of their culture. But it was extremely difficult to imagine finding a medicine woman. To my knowledge, there have been no books written about a medicine woman, and they are even more hidden than the medicine men.

Continuing our search, we visited the small town that was close to our land. This was Cortez, Colorado, a common stopping point for visitors to the Mesa Verde National Park. In Cortez we found a museum that hosted weekly lectures and traditional dances. I introduced myself to the director of the museum, Ann Chambers, and asked if she knew any medicine women. She immediately declared that there was a remarkable medicine woman who I should meet. This was Walking Thunder. She could only tell me that she lived in the Two Grey Hills area. Walking Thunder had no address or phone number. I had to go to the reservation and track her down.

Subsequently, we spent several days trying to find Walking Thunder. We were eventually told the color of her pickup truck and we drove throughout the dirt back roads hoping to find it. We stopped at every house and asked if they knew her. Finally, we arrived at her home at the base of a canyon. There her son, Darryle, warmly greeted us and said she would return that evening.

We met and decided to see whether the Creator had brought us together for some sacred work. She consulted with her elders and her family, and finally they decided to put me through a series of ceremonies. Their tradition asks that the details of these ceremonies not be disclosed, but I can say that I witnessed firsthand the special relationship she has with Mother Nature. Her prayers can awaken the thunder and cause the holy wind to enter the room. In her ceremonies, my body has turned blue, shaken wildly, as my eyes observed lightning fill the room. I say these things as a testimony of her relationship with the Holy Ones.

I can also testify that she is an effective healer. When we first met, she almost immediately said, "I want to heal your asthma." This was a condition I had suffered from since childhood when I would go into the hospital several times a year with severe bronchial distress. At the time I met her, I was on a high level of medical care, taking several kinds of inhalers and medications. I had tried numerous complementary medical interventions from all over the world, from African ritual to Chinese medicine, and nothing had helped. I was at the stage where no placebo effect could work for me and the severity of my asthma was escalating to becoming a major health crisis. She doctored me and gave me a small medicine pouch filled with herbs. Her instructions were to take a small pinch of the herbs whenever I felt that I needed it. As difficult as this is to believe, my asthma was under control within 24 hours. Since that day, I have never taken a single dose of medicine and I have thrown away my inhalers. This was unquestionably a miracle in my life that I cannot deny.

When my mother-in-law was in the final stage of stomach cancer, one of her last requests was to see Walking Thunder. We put her in a wheelchair and took her to the reservation. Barely able to walk, unable to eat, and yellowed with jaundice, Ruth sat on a sacred sandpainting and was prayed over in the traditional way. She emerged with a new found vitality and a glow of peace on her face that we had never seen before. She insisted on visiting Santa Fe and there she ate three meals a day and walked every day for a week. She then made trips to visit her grandchildren, her friends and relatives, and it wasn't until months later that she peacefully went on to the next world, keeping a picture of Walking Thunder next to her bed.

Walking Thunder takes her orders from the Creator. Be careful if you try to get in the way of doing the work she has been called to perform. She is one of the most outspoken persons I have ever met.

When she enters a community meeting, everyone knows that she will speak her mind if she is so moved. It surprises no one that she is called Walking Thunder.

When my colleague, Nancy Connor, brought her to the World Forum in New York City, a meeting that brought together leaders from all over the world, Walking Thunder came with her gourd box and her medicines, ready to pray over anyone who was hungry for being touched by spirit. In New York, she prayed for a professional wrestler, a financial executive and his family, and elder healers from Hawaii and Senegal. Although she was out late at night, sitting in Rodney Dangerfield's Comedy Club, laughing louder than anyone else in the room, the next day she'd be sitting on the floor, praying away, blessing and healing others who came for help.

Walking Thunder never misses an opportunity to exercise her healing practice. She is even known for giving help to truck drivers via her CB radio. "This is Walking Thunder, over and out." I was particularly impressed by one of the ways she teaches her medicine way. She will take her student with her to a nearby town like Shiprock or Farmington or Gallup, New Mexico, and locate a skid-row drunk passed out on the side of the road. She'll pull over, pick up the alcohol afflicted person and take him back to her hogan. There she'll teach the apprentice how to make that sick man well. She's that determined to teach and heal.

In spite of her strong will and energy, she has a tender heart and is sometimes hurt by the jealousies of other medicine men. What keeps her going are the dreams that come to her when she needs them and the constant encouragement of her elder teachers, from the past and present, who insist that she follow the Creator, not the rules of men. Because of her teachings, she continues to get up each morning and take that first step, praying for a walk in beauty.

Walking Thunder introduced me to her teacher, He Who Walks Away. I discovered that he was the medicine man I had seen in my dreams. He wore a red scarf around his head and not only held the eagle feathers, but could call the eagles down from the sky. He quietly held my hand and went into a light trance, as other Diné medicine people had done, and performed a vision on me, saying that I was a clear crystal. He said he may have seen me before in an earlier vision in his life and offered to teach me his knowledge. He encouraged Walking Thunder to teach me the old ways.

I experienced firsthand the ceremonies I had earlier dreamed and the old man gave me a song, a song about entering into beauty. This is how I was introduced to the medicine ways of the Diné. There are militant traditionalists who oppose anything being said about their practices and they particularly fight against any white person being told these things. However, Walking Thunder's ceremonials, prayers, and counsel from her elders, directed her to tell her story to me and telling some, but not all, of the ways of Diné healing. She believes that the Creator has asked her to do this, whether she wants to or not.

In our work together, some people, including those who practice the witchery way, have tried to impede this project. We have had curses put upon us and both of us have been confronted face-to-face with strong challenges. Together, we have faced these storms and they have made us stronger. The work was done in response to a calling that touched many of us and it stands as an offering and testimony to a way of life that walks in respectful relationship to the Creator and seeks to find beauty in every waking moment.

After she finished telling me her life story, I took her to the land I had dreamed about years before. There she found her medicines growing in abundance. At the canyon's rim, she prayed and announced that we were standing on a holy place. It was old Anasazi ground, perfectly designed by nature for ceremony and seeking vision, and advised me that it would be a good place for elder medicine people to recharge their spiritual batteries. She went on to explain how the

Canyon rim traditional way in which a medicine person found a sacred piece of land was to find a piece of petrified wood that would lead them to it. I immediately remembered how my grandfather had brought me to that land through my dreaming about a piece of petrified wood. I stood there seized by a profound awareness of mystery.

We dedicate this book to the teachings of Walking Thunder's late husband, David Peters; and to the late Ruth Jenson, whose life spirit proved that we are all children who belong to the same Creator.

References

Aberle, D. *The Peyote Religion Among the Navajo*. Chicago: Aldine, 1966.

Beck, Peggy V. & Anna L. Walters, eds. *The Sacred: Ways of Knowing, Sources of Life*. Tsaile, AZ: Navajo Community College Press, 1977.

Benally, Herbert. "Diné Bo'ohoo'aah Bindii': Navajo Philosophy of Learning." *Diné Béiina: A Journal of Navajo Life*, vol. 1, no. 1, Spring 1987.

Farella, John. *The Main Stalk*. Tucson: University of Arizona Press, 1990.

Faris, James C. *The Nightway*. Albuquerque: University of New Mexico Press, 1989.

Gilpin, L. *The Enduring Navaho*. Austin: University of Texas Press, 1968.

Griffin-Pierce, T. *Earth Is My Mother, Sky Is My Father: Space, Time, and Astronomy in Navajo Sandpainting*. Albuquerque: University of New Mexico Press, 1992.

Haile, Father Berard. *Waterway: A Navajo Ceremonial Myth Told by Black Mustache Circle*. Flagstaff: Museum of Northern Arizona Press, 1979.

————. *Legend of the Ghostway Ritual and Suckingway*. Saint Michaels, AZ: St. Michaels' Press, 1950.

————. "Navajo Chantways and Ceremonials." *American Anthropologist*, vol. 40, no. 4, 1938, 639–652.

Haile, Father Berard & M. Oakes. *Beautyway: A Navajo Ceremonial*. New York: Bollingen Foundation, 1957.

Klah, Hosteen. *Myth of Mountain Chant and Beauty Chant*. Santa Fe: Museum of Navajo Ceremonial Art, 1951.

————. *Wind Chant and Feather Chant*. Santa Fe: Museum of Navajo Ceremonial Art, 1946.

————. *Tleji or Yeibechai Myth*. Santa Fe: Museum of Navajo Ceremonial Art, 1938.

————. *Texts of the Navajo Creation Chants*. Collected and translated by Dr. Harry Hoijer. Cambridge: Peabody Museum of Harvard University, 1929.

Klukhohn, Clyde & Leland C. Wyman. "An Introduction to Navajo Chant Practice." Memoirs of the American Anthropological Association, Menasha, WS: American Anthropological Association, 1940. *Supplement to American Anthropologist*, vol. 42, no. 2, Part 2.

Kluckholm, Clyde & Dorothea Leighton. *The Navajo*. Cambridge: Harvard University Press, 1946.

LaBarre, Weston. *The Peyote Cult*. Hamden, CT: Shoe String Press, 1938 and 1964.

Leighton, Alexander H. & Dorothea C. Leighton. "Gregorio the Hand-Trembler: A Psychological Personality Study of a Navaho Indian." Papers of the Peabody Museum of

American Archaeology and Ethnology. Cambridge, MA: Harvard University, vol. 40, no. 1, 1949, p. 158.

————. *Lucky: The Navajo Singer*. Albuquerque: University of New Mexico Press, 1992.

————. *The Navajo Door*. Cambridge: Harvard University Press, 1944.

Link, Margaret S. *The Pollen Path*. Walnut, CA: Kiva Publishing, 1998.

Locke, R.F. *The Book of the Navajo*. Los Angeles: Mankind Publishing Co., 1976.

Matthews, Washington. "The Mountain Chant." Annual Report of the Bureau of American Ethnology. Vol. 5, 1883–84, Washington, D.C.: U.S. Government Printing Office.

————. Washington Matthews, *Navajo Legend*, vol. 5 of Memoirs of the American Folklore Society, Cambridge, MA: The Riverside Press, 1897.

————. *The Night Chant: A Navajo Ceremony*. New York: American Museum of Natural History, 1902.

McNeley, James K. *Holy Wind*. Tucson: University of Arizona Press, 1981.

————. "Imminent Mind in Navajo Philosophy and Batesonian Holistic Science." *Diné Be'lina: A Journal of Navajo Life*, vol. 1, no. 1, Spring 1987.

Moon, Sheila. *A Magic Dwells: A Poetic and Psychological Study of the Navajo Emergence Myth*. San Francisco: Guild for Psychological Studies Publishing House, 1970.

Newcomb, Franc Johnson, S. Fishler, & M.C. Wheelwright. *A Study of Navajo Symbolism*. Cambridge: Peabody Museum of Harvard University, 1956.

Newcomb, Franc Johnson, & Gladys Reichard. *Sandpaintings of the Navajo Shooting Chant*. New York: Dover Publications, 1975.

Newcomb, Franc Johnson. *Hosteen Klah: Navajo Medicine Man and Sand Painter*. Norman: University of Oklahoma Press, 1964.

————. *Navajo Folk Tales*. Santa Fe: Museum of Navajo Ceremonial Art. 1967.

————. *Navajo Omens and Taboos*. Santa Fe: The Rydal Press, 1940.

Oaks, Maud, & Joseph Campbell. *Where the Two Came to The Father*. Princeton, NJ: Princeton University Press, 1989.

O'Bryan, Aileen. "The Diné: Origin Myths of the Navajo Indians." Bureau of American Ethnology, Bulletin 163. Washington, D.C.: Smithsonian Institution, 1956.

Ortiz, Alfonso, ed. *Handbook of North American Indians*, vol. 10. Washington, D.C.: U.S. Government Printing Office, 1983.

Parezo, N. ed. *Navajo Sandpainting: From Religious Act to Commercial Art*. Albuquerque:

University of New Mexico Press, 1983.

Reichard, Gladys A. "Navajo Religion: A Study of Symbolism." *Bollingen Series*,
no. 18. Princeton, NJ: Princeton University Press, 1963.

———. *Navajo Medicine Man Sandpaintings*. New York: Dover Publications, 1977.

———. *Navajo Religion*. New York: Pantheon Books, 1950.

———. *Social Life of the Navajo Indians*. New York: Columbia University Press, 1978.

———. *The Story of the Navajo Hail Chant*. New York: Columbia University Press, 1944.

Roessel, R. *Women in Navajo Society*. Rough Rock, AZ: Navajo Resource Center, 1981.

Sandner, Donald. *Navajo Symbols of Healing*. Rochester, VT: Healing Arts Press, 1991.

Schevill, Margaret E. *Beautiful on the Earth*. Santa Fe: Hazel Dreis Editions, 1947.

Stevenson, James. "The Ceremonial of Hasjelti Dailjis: Mythical Sandpainting of the Navajo
Indians." Annual Report of the Bureau of American Ethnology. vol. 8, 1886–87, Washington,
D.C.: U.S. Government Printing Office.

Villaseñor, David. *Tapestries in Sand: The Spirit of Indian Sandpainting*.
Happy Camp, CA: Naturegraph Pub., 1963.

Wheelwright, Mary C. *The Myth and Prayers of the Great Star Chant and the Myth
of the Coyote Chant*. Santa Fe: Museum of Navajo Ceremonial Art, 1956.

Witherspoon, Gary. *Language and Art in the Navajo Universe*. Ann Arbor: University
of Michigan Press, 1977.

Wyman, Leland C. *Navajo Sandpainting*. Colorado Springs: The Taylor Museum, 1980.

———. *Blessingway*. Tucson: University of Arizona Press, 1970.

———. *The Windways of the Navajo*. Colorado Springs: The Taylor Museum Press, 1962.

———. *The Red Antway of the Navajo*. Santa Fe: Museum of Navajo Ceremonial Art, 1965.

———. *The Sandpaintings of the Kayenta Navajo*. Albuquerque: University of New Mexico
Press, 1952.

Yazzie, E. *Navajo History*. Vols. 1–3. Rough Rock, AZ: Rough Rock Community
Schools Press, early 1980s.

———. *Navajo History*. Many Farms, AZ: Navajo Community College Press, 1971.

Zolbrod, Paul. *Diné Bahané, The Navajo Creation Story*. Albuquerque:
University of New Mexico Press, 1984.

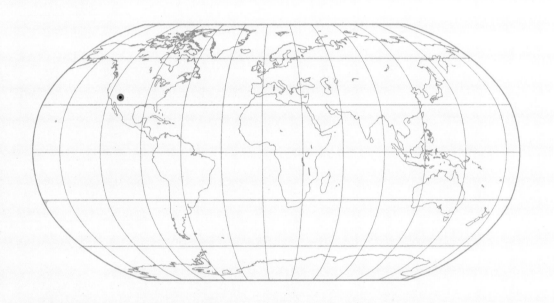